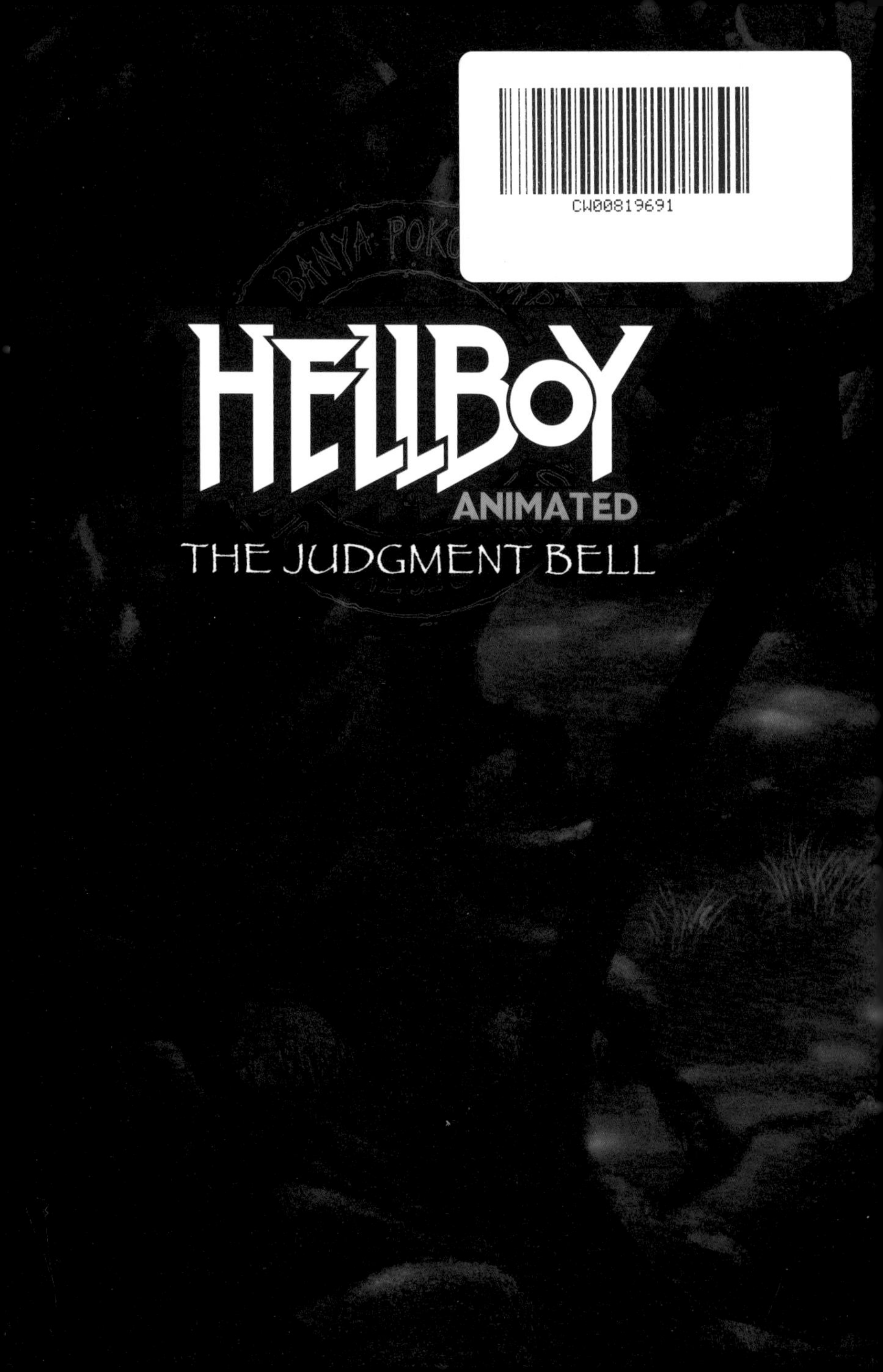

HELLBOY ANIMATED

THE JUDGMENT BELL

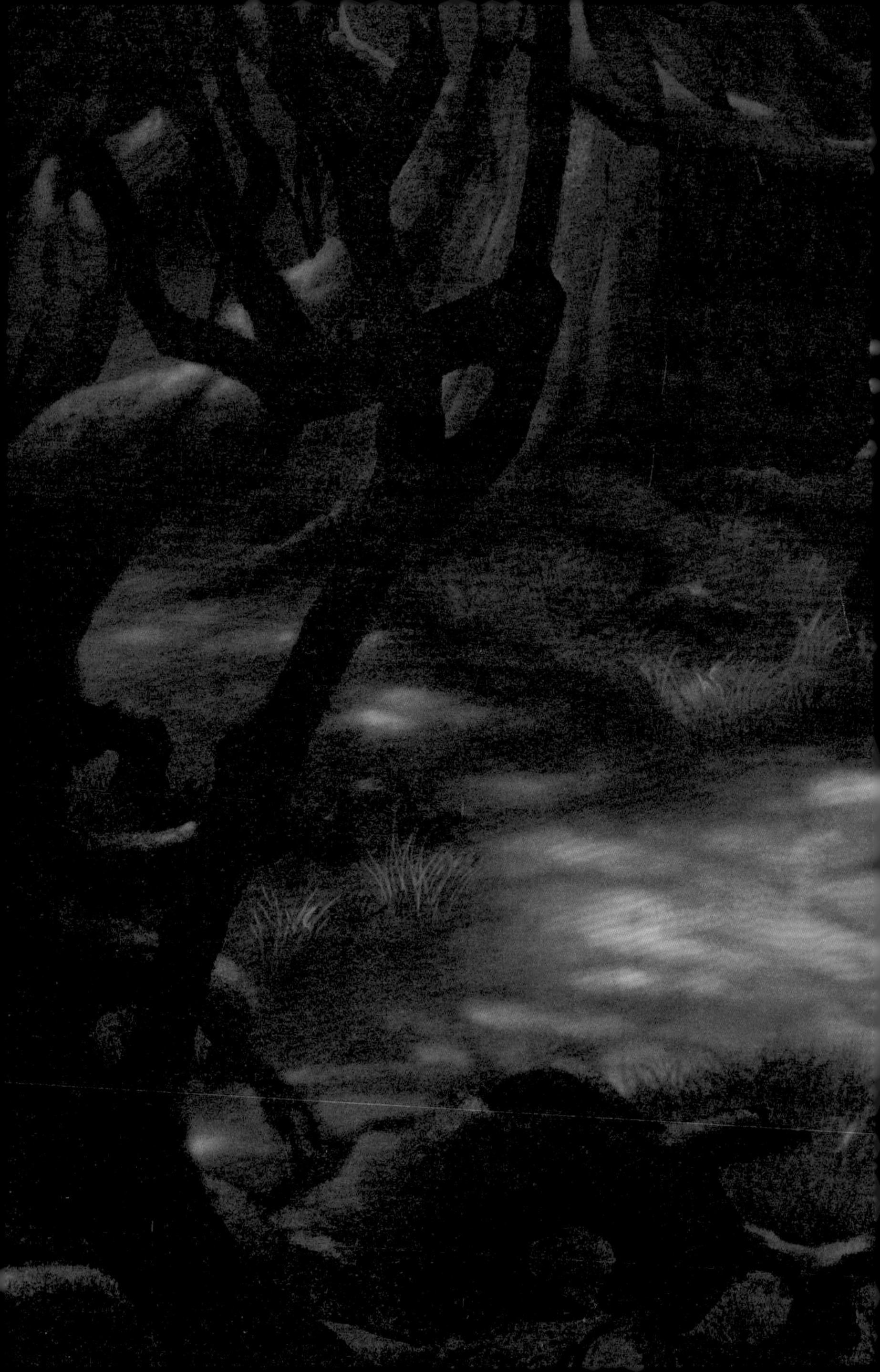

HELLBOY
ANIMATED

THE JUDGMENT BELL

Story by JIM PASCOE

Art by RICK LACY

Colors by MICHELLE MADSEN

Letters by BLAMBOT'S NATE PIEKOS

PINUP

Art by MIKE MIGNOLA

Colors by DAVE STEWART

MECHANICAL MONSTERS

Story and Art by TAD STONES

Colors by MICHELLE MADSEN

Letters by BLAMBOT'S NATE PIEKOS

Cover by ERIC POWELL

Hellboy and the B.P.R.D. created by MIKE MIGNOLA

Dark Horse Books®

Publisher MIKE RICHARDSON

Editor MATT DRYER

Assistant Editor RACHEL EDIDIN

Designer KEITH WOOD

Special Thanks to MIKE and CHRISTINE MIGNOLA, SCOTT ALLIE, DAVE STEWART, GUY DAVIS, JOHN ARCUDI, TAD STONES, and DAN JACKSON

Hellboy Animated: The Judgment Bell, June 2007. Published by Dark Horse Comics, Inc., 10956 SE Main Street, Milwaukie, Oregon 97222.

Published by
Dark Horse Books
A division of Dark Horse Comics, Inc.
10956 SE Main Street
Milwaukie, OR 97222

darkhorse.com

To find a comics shop in your area,
call the Comic Shop Locator Service toll-free at 1-888-266-4226

First Edition: June 2007
ISBN-10: 1-59307-799-8
ISBN-13: 978-1-59307-799-0

1 3 5 7 9 10 8 6 4 2

Printed in the United States of America

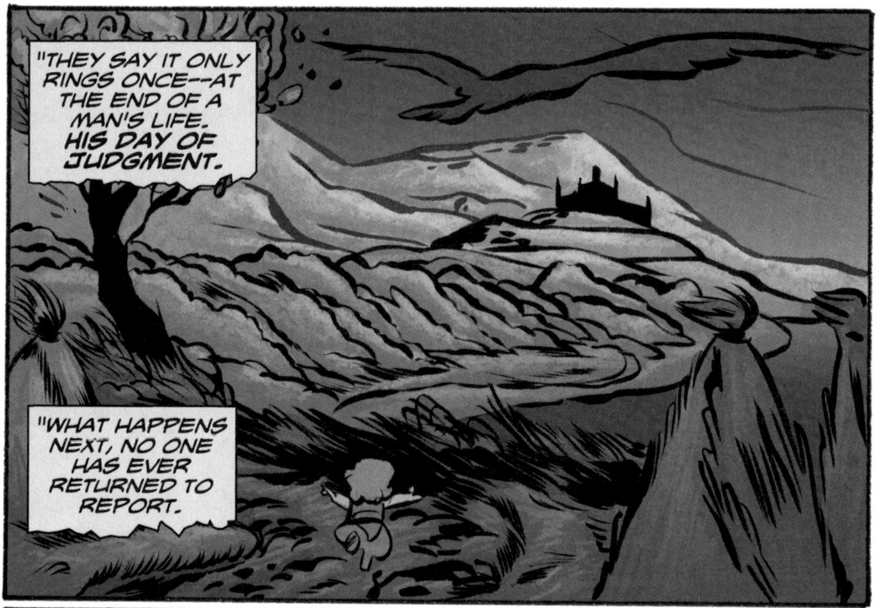
"THEY SAY IT ONLY RINGS ONCE--AT THE END OF A MAN'S LIFE. HIS DAY OF JUDGMENT.
"WHAT HAPPENS NEXT, NO ONE HAS EVER RETURNED TO REPORT.

THE JUDGMENT BELL

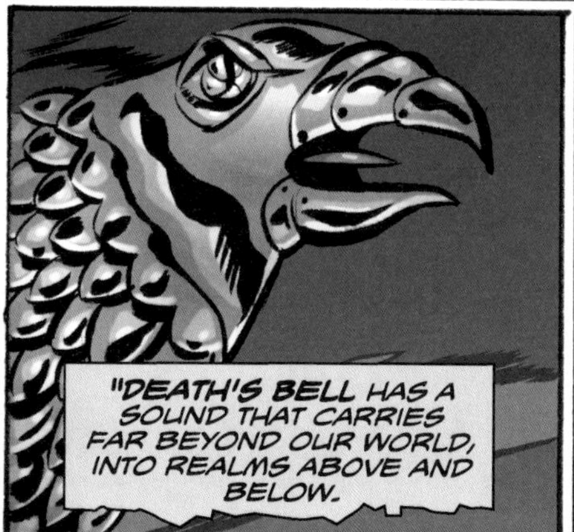
"DEATH'S BELL HAS A SOUND THAT CARRIES FAR BEYOND OUR WORLD, INTO REALMS ABOVE AND BELOW.

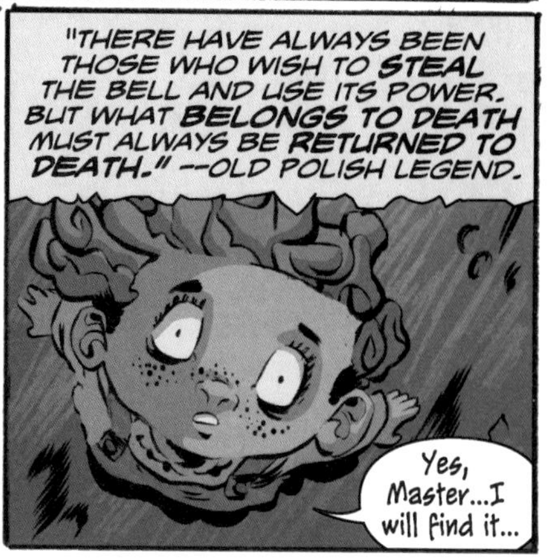
"THERE HAVE ALWAYS BEEN THOSE WHO WISH TO STEAL THE BELL AND USE ITS POWER. BUT WHAT BELONGS TO DEATH MUST ALWAYS BE RETURNED TO DEATH." --OLD POLISH LEGEND.
Yes, Master...I will find it...

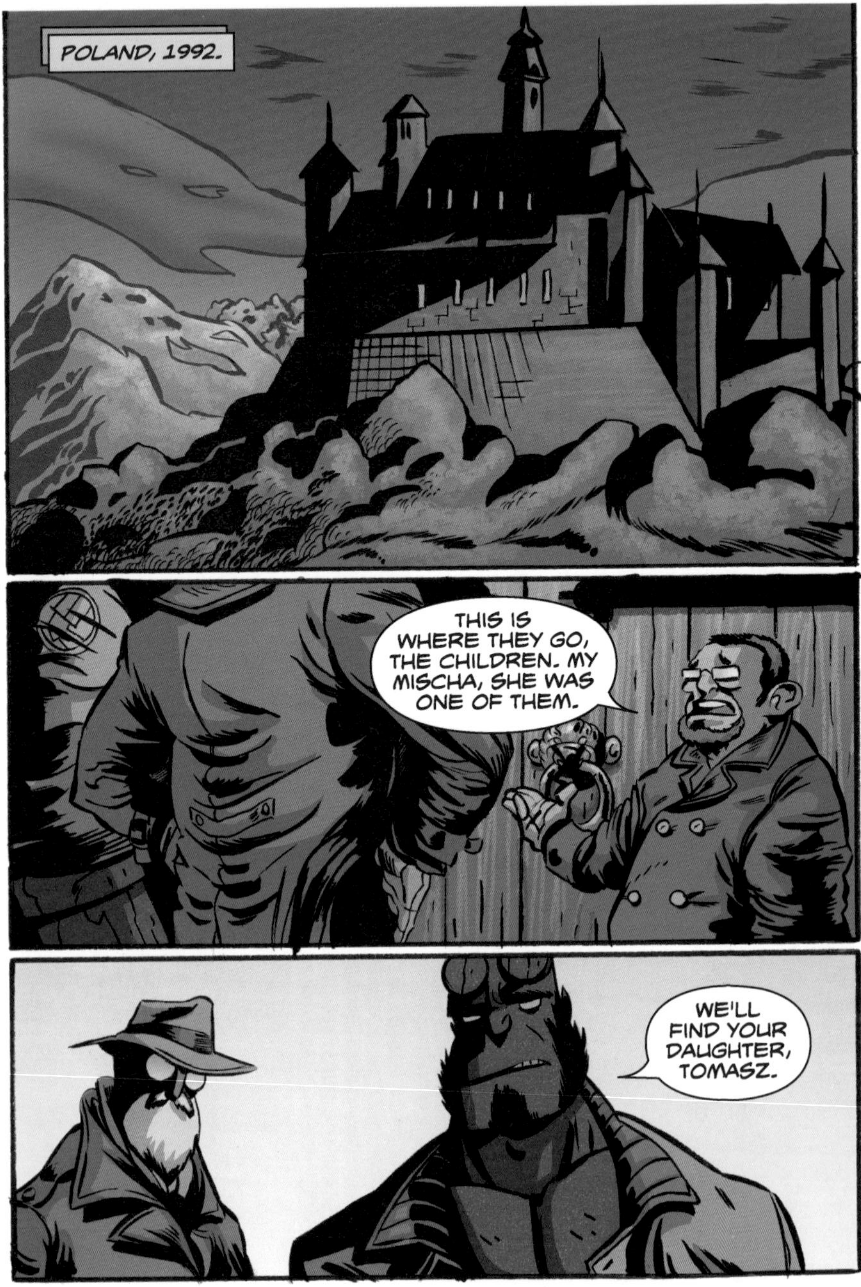
POLAND, 1992.
THIS IS WHERE THEY GO, THE CHILDREN. MY MISCHA, SHE WAS ONE OF THEM.
WE'LL FIND YOUR DAUGHTER, TOMASZ.

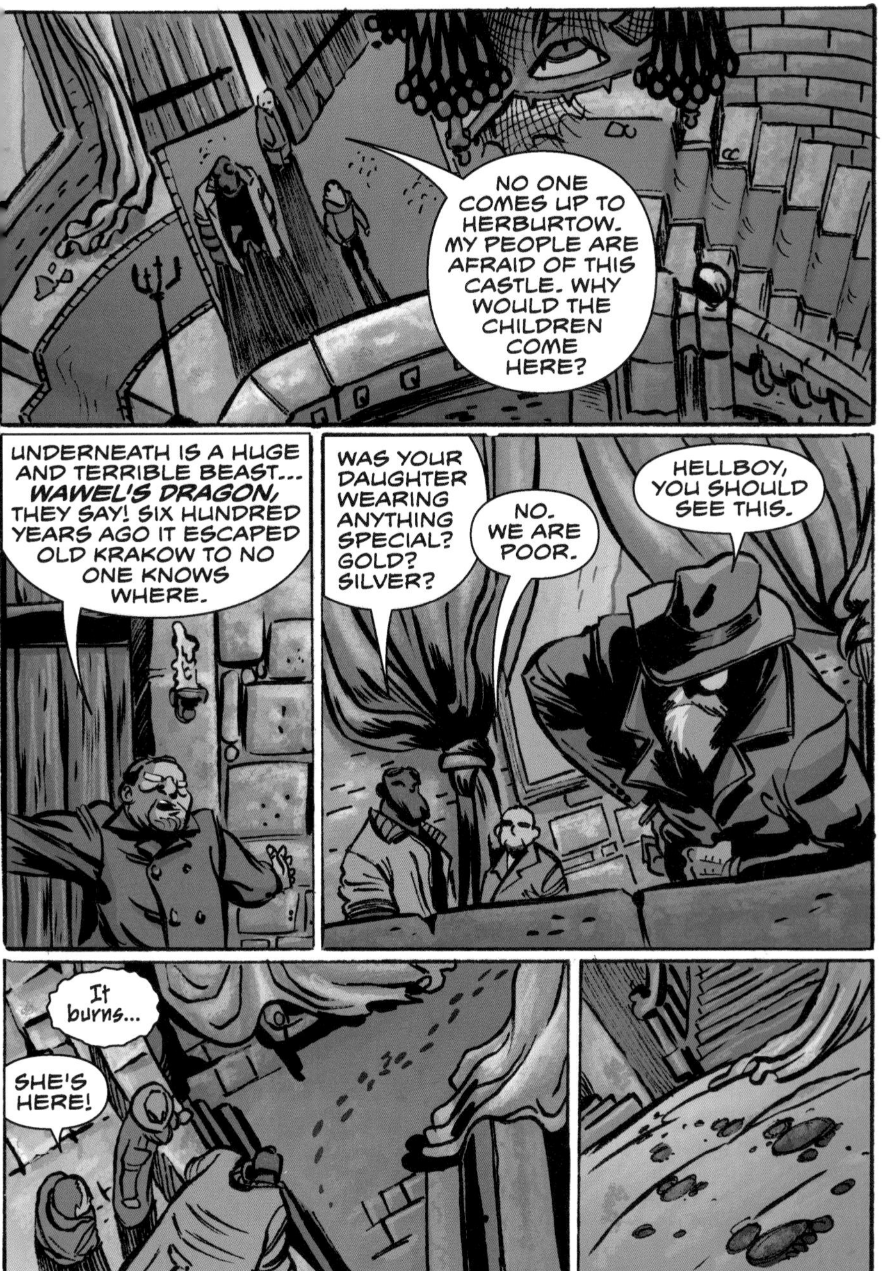
NO ONE COMES UP TO HERBURTOW. MY PEOPLE ARE AFRAID OF THIS CASTLE. WHY WOULD THE CHILDREN COME HERE?
UNDERNEATH IS A HUGE AND TERRIBLE BEAST... ***WAWEL'S DRAGON,*** THEY SAY! SIX HUNDRED YEARS AGO IT ESCAPED OLD KRAKOW TO NO ONE KNOWS WHERE.
WAS YOUR DAUGHTER WEARING ANYTHING SPECIAL? GOLD? SILVER?
NO. WE ARE POOR.
HELLBOY, YOU SHOULD SEE THIS.
It burns...
SHE'S HERE!

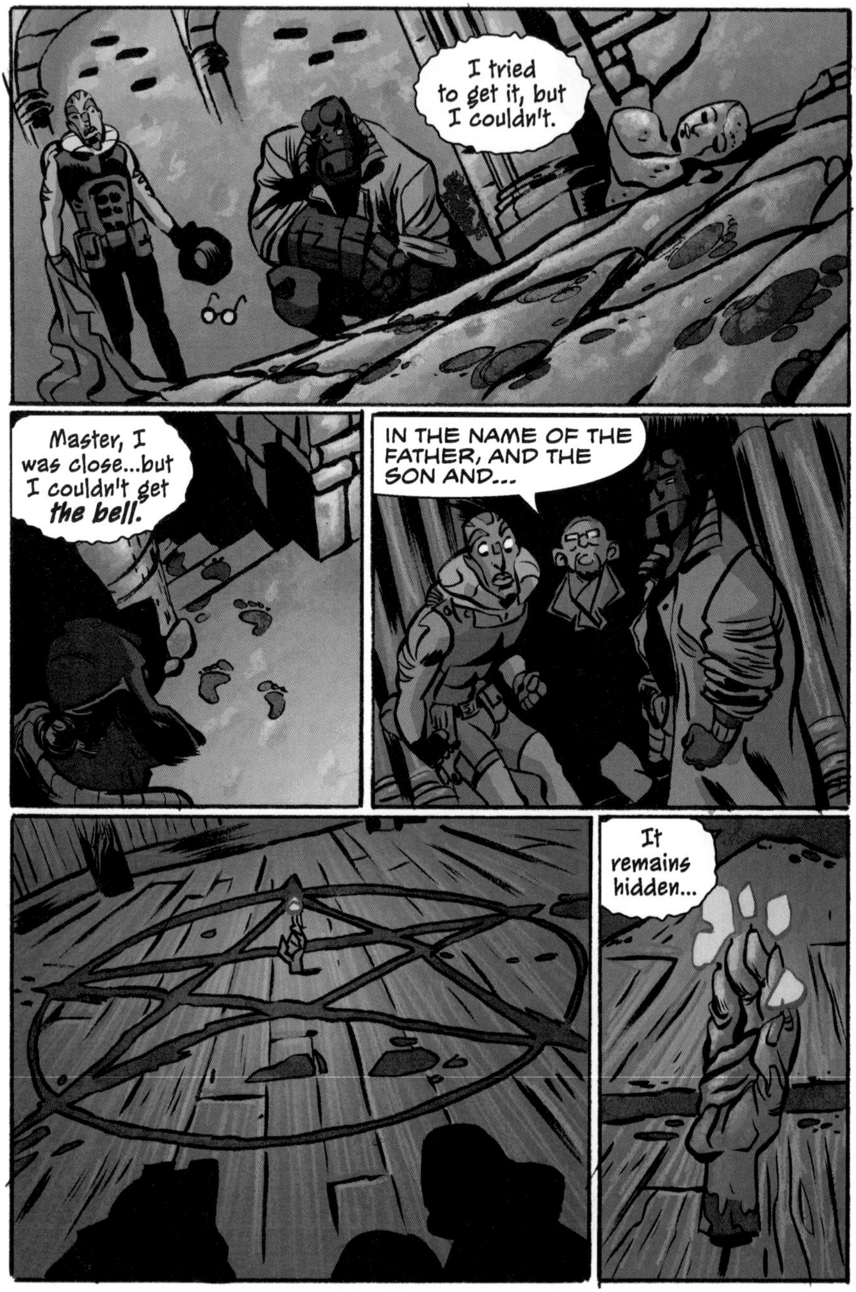
I tried to get it, but I couldn't.
Master, I was close...but I couldn't get *the bell.*
IN THE NAME OF THE FATHER, AND THE SON AND...
It remains hidden...

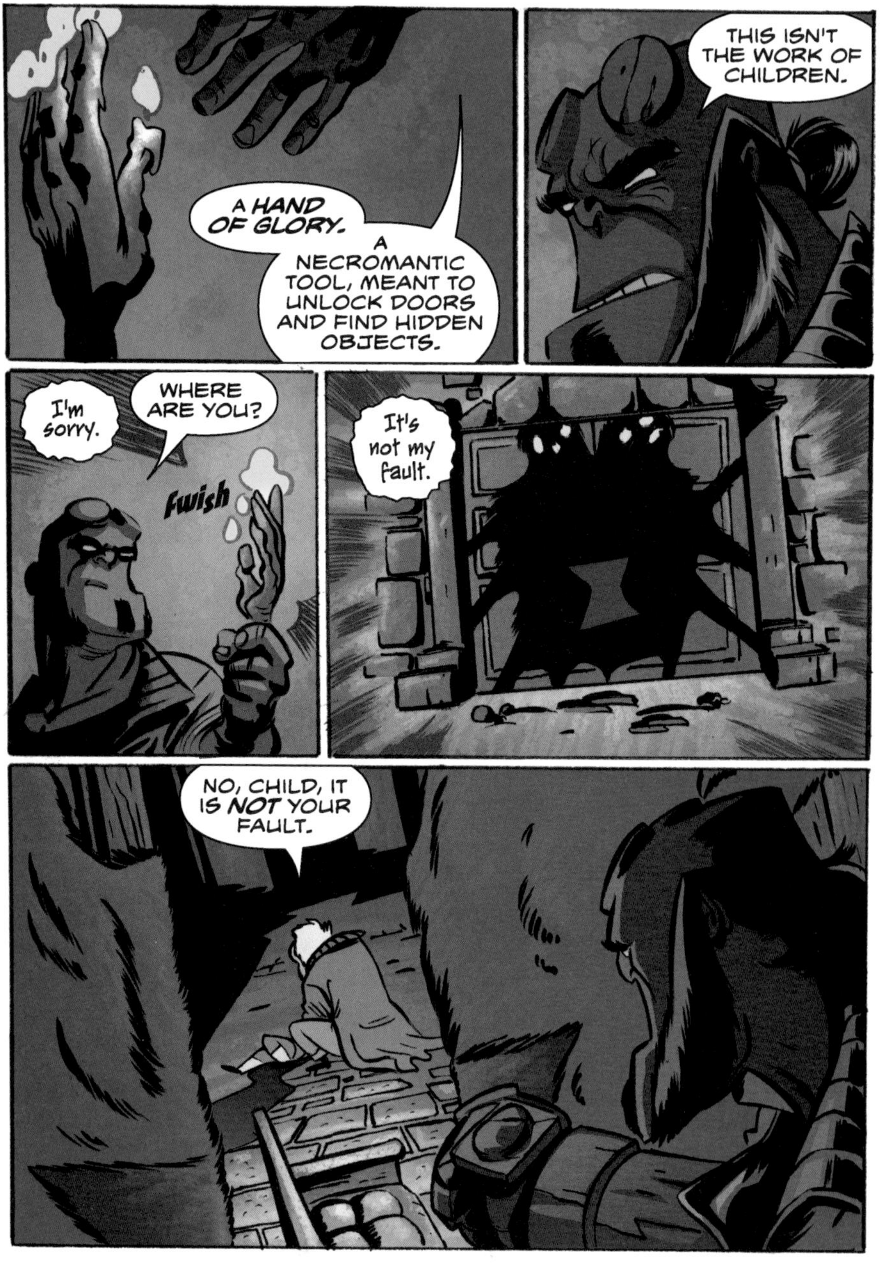
A HAND OF GLORY.
A NECROMANTIC TOOL, MEANT TO UNLOCK DOORS AND FIND HIDDEN OBJECTS.
THIS ISN'T THE WORK OF CHILDREN.
WHERE ARE YOU?
I'm sorry.
fwish
It's not my fault.
NO, CHILD, IT IS NOT YOUR FAULT.

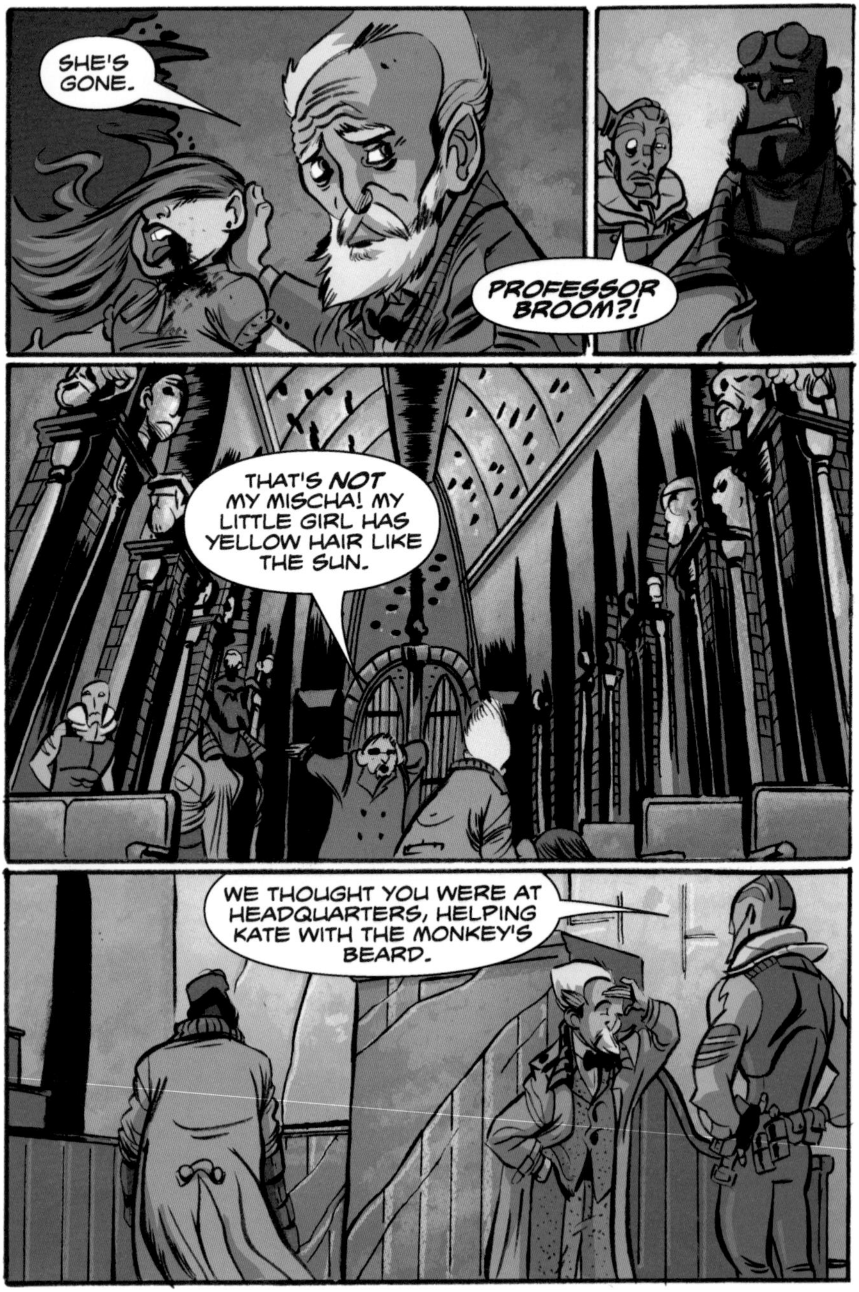
SHE'S GONE.
PROFESSOR BROOM?!
THAT'S NOT MY MISCHA! MY LITTLE GIRL HAS YELLOW HAIR LIKE THE SUN.
WE THOUGHT YOU WERE AT HEADQUARTERS, HELPING KATE WITH THE MONKEY'S BEARD.

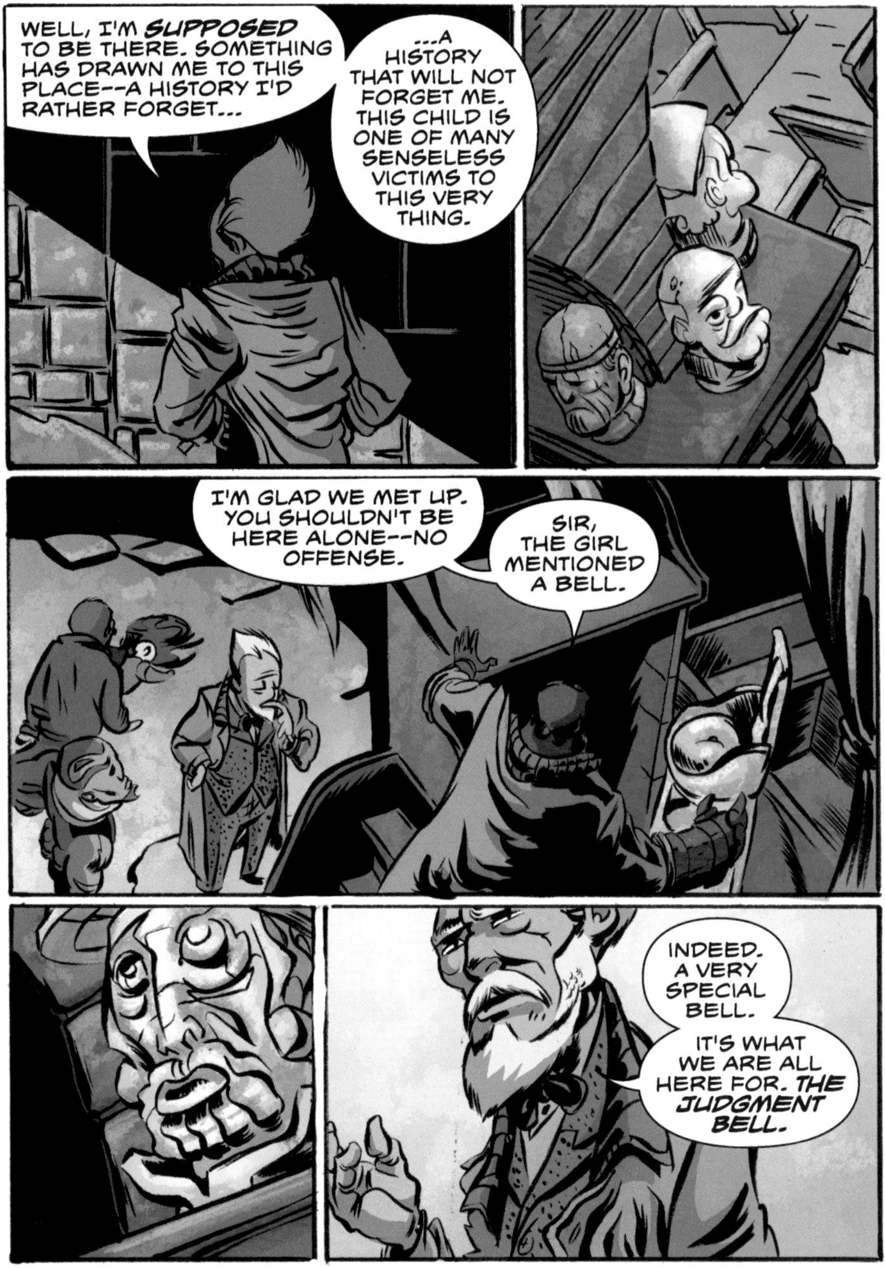
WELL, I'M SUPPOSED TO BE THERE. SOMETHING HAS DRAWN ME TO THIS PLACE--A HISTORY I'D RATHER FORGET...
...A HISTORY THAT WILL NOT FORGET ME. THIS CHILD IS ONE OF MANY SENSELESS VICTIMS TO THIS VERY THING.
I'M GLAD WE MET UP. YOU SHOULDN'T BE HERE ALONE--NO OFFENSE.
SIR, THE GIRL MENTIONED A BELL.
INDEED. A VERY SPECIAL BELL.
IT'S WHAT WE ARE ALL HERE FOR. THE JUDGMENT BELL.

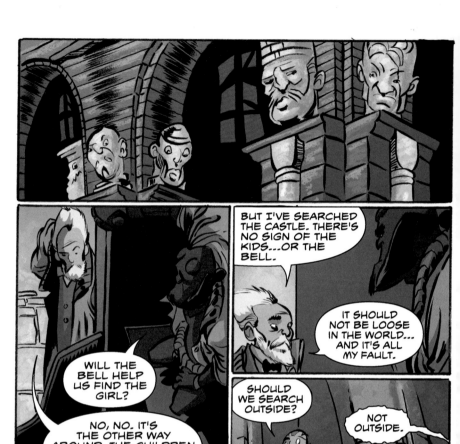

BUT I'VE SEARCHED THE CASTLE. THERE'S NO SIGN OF THE KIDS...OR THE BELL.

IT SHOULD NOT BE LOOSE IN THE WORLD... AND IT'S ALL MY FAULT.

WILL THE BELL HELP US FIND THE GIRL?

NO, NO. IT'S THE OTHER WAY AROUND. THE CHILDREN WERE DRAWN TO THIS CASTLE TO FIND THE BELL.

SHOULD WE SEARCH OUTSIDE?

NOT OUTSIDE.

INSIDE.

THE DOORS!

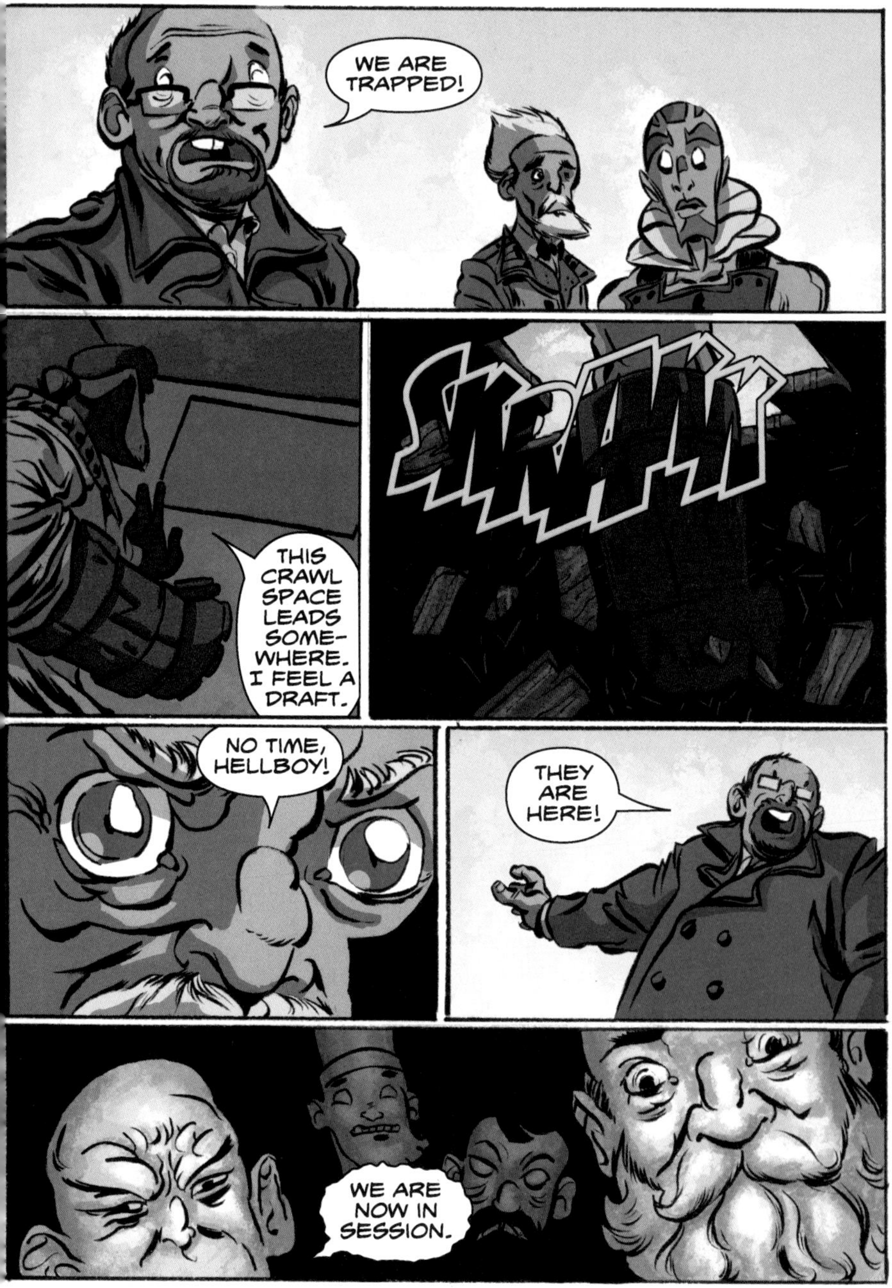
WE ARE TRAPPED!
THIS CRAWL SPACE LEADS SOME- WHERE. I FEEL A DRAFT.
NO TIME, HELLBOY!
THEY ARE HERE!
WE ARE NOW IN SESSION.

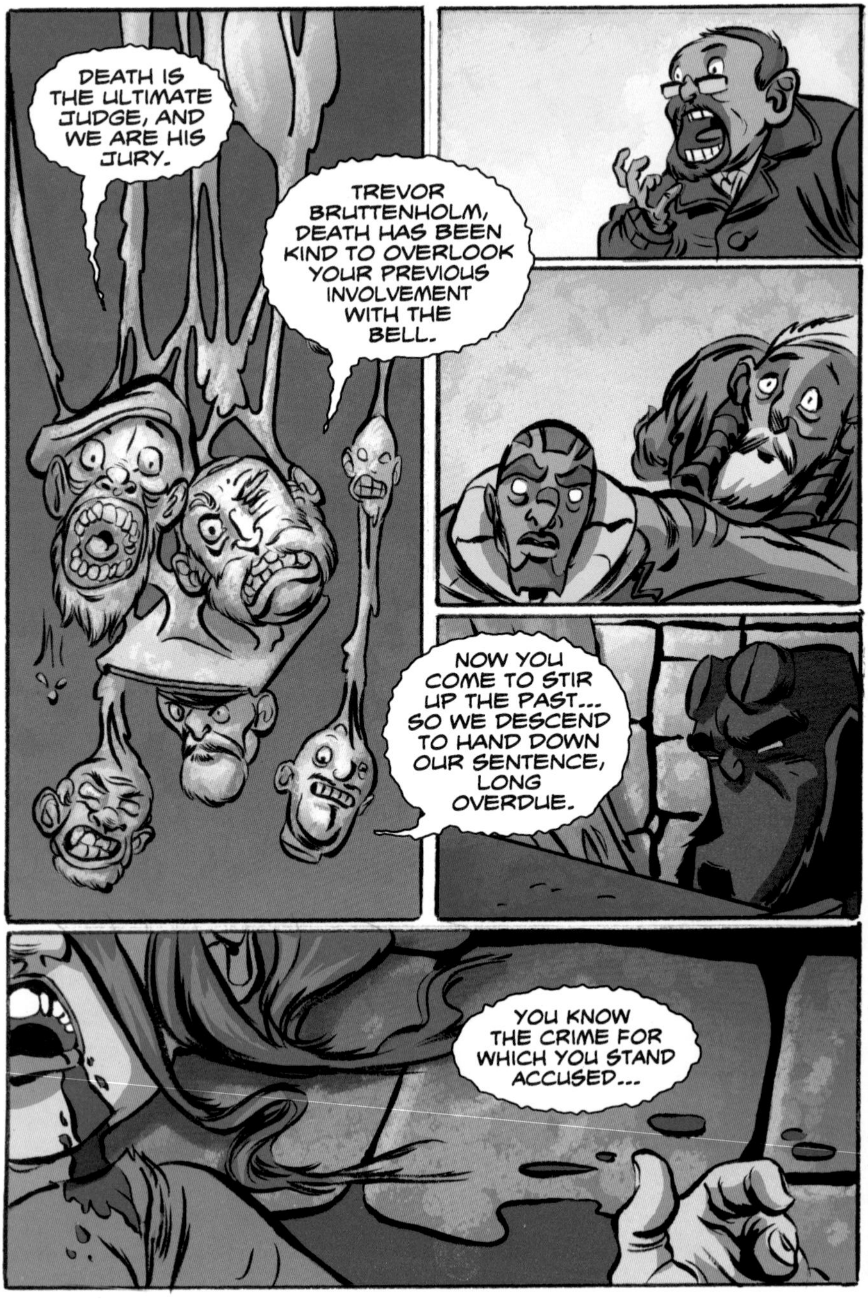
DEATH IS THE ULTIMATE JUDGE, AND WE ARE HIS JURY.
TREVOR BRUTTENHOLM, DEATH HAS BEEN KIND TO OVERLOOK YOUR PREVIOUS INVOLVEMENT WITH THE BELL.
NOW YOU COME TO STIR UP THE PAST... SO WE DESCEND TO HAND DOWN OUR SENTENCE, LONG OVERDUE.
YOU KNOW THE CRIME FOR WHICH YOU STAND ACCUSED...

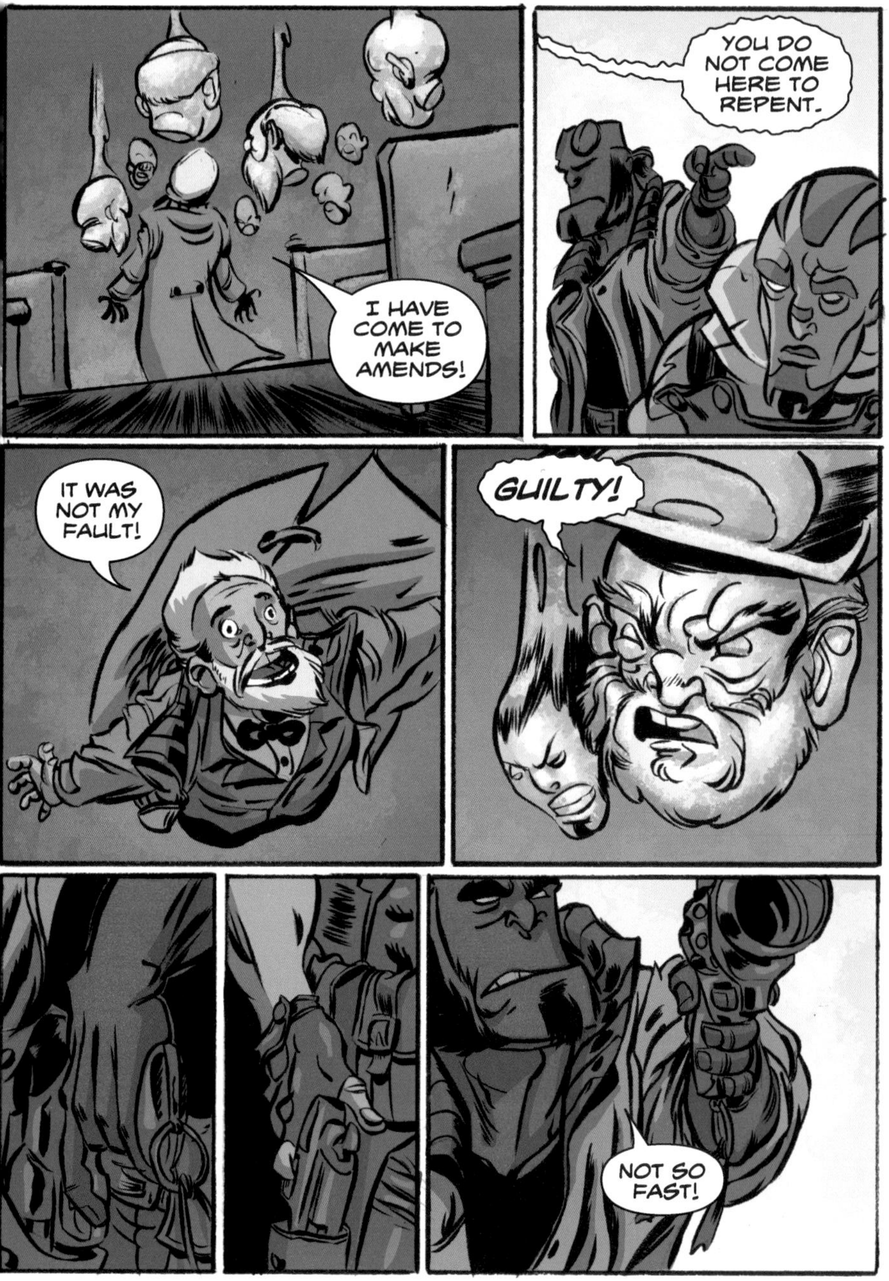
I HAVE COME TO MAKE AMENDS!
YOU DO NOT COME HERE TO REPENT.
IT WAS NOT MY FAULT!
GUILTY!
NOT SO FAST!

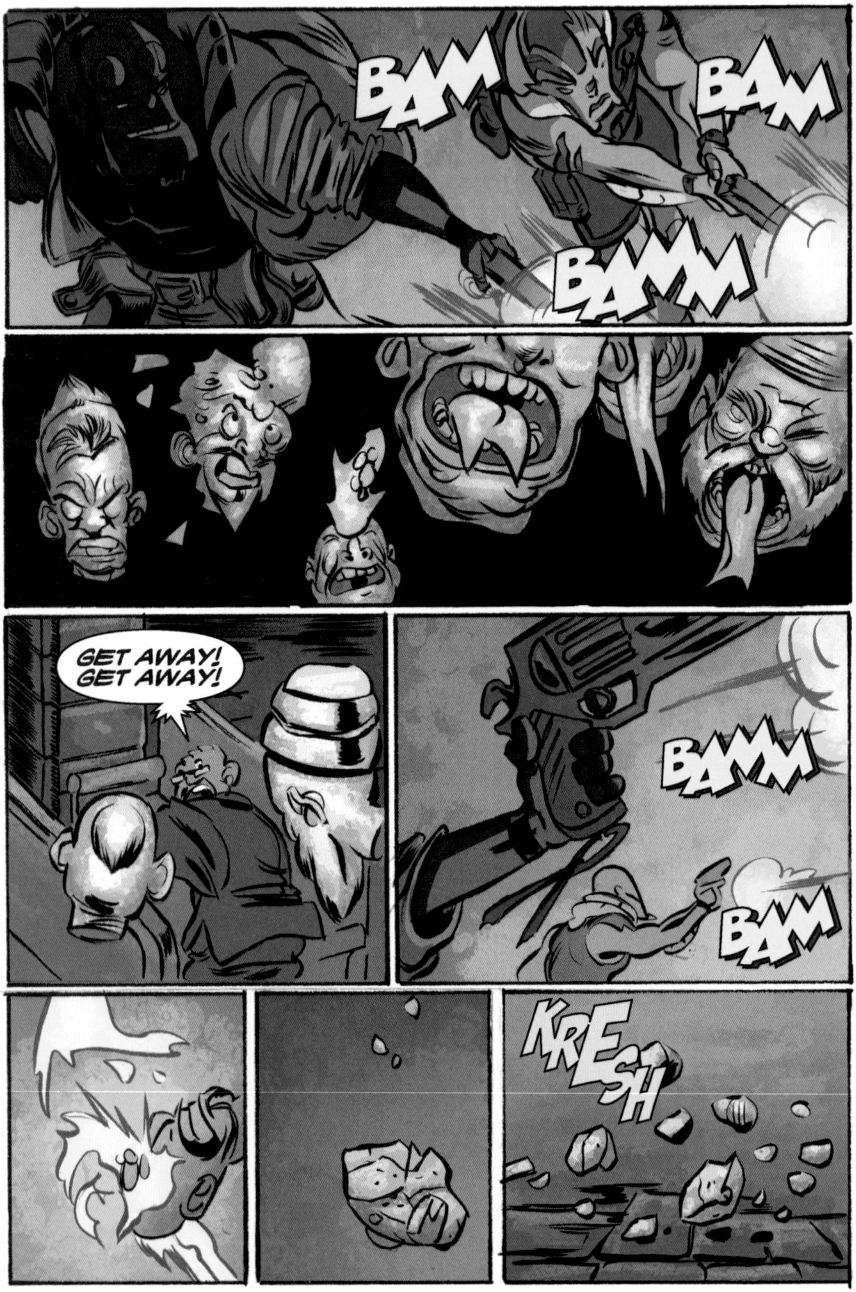
BAM
BAM
BAMM
GET AWAY! GET AWAY!
BAMM
BAM
KRESH

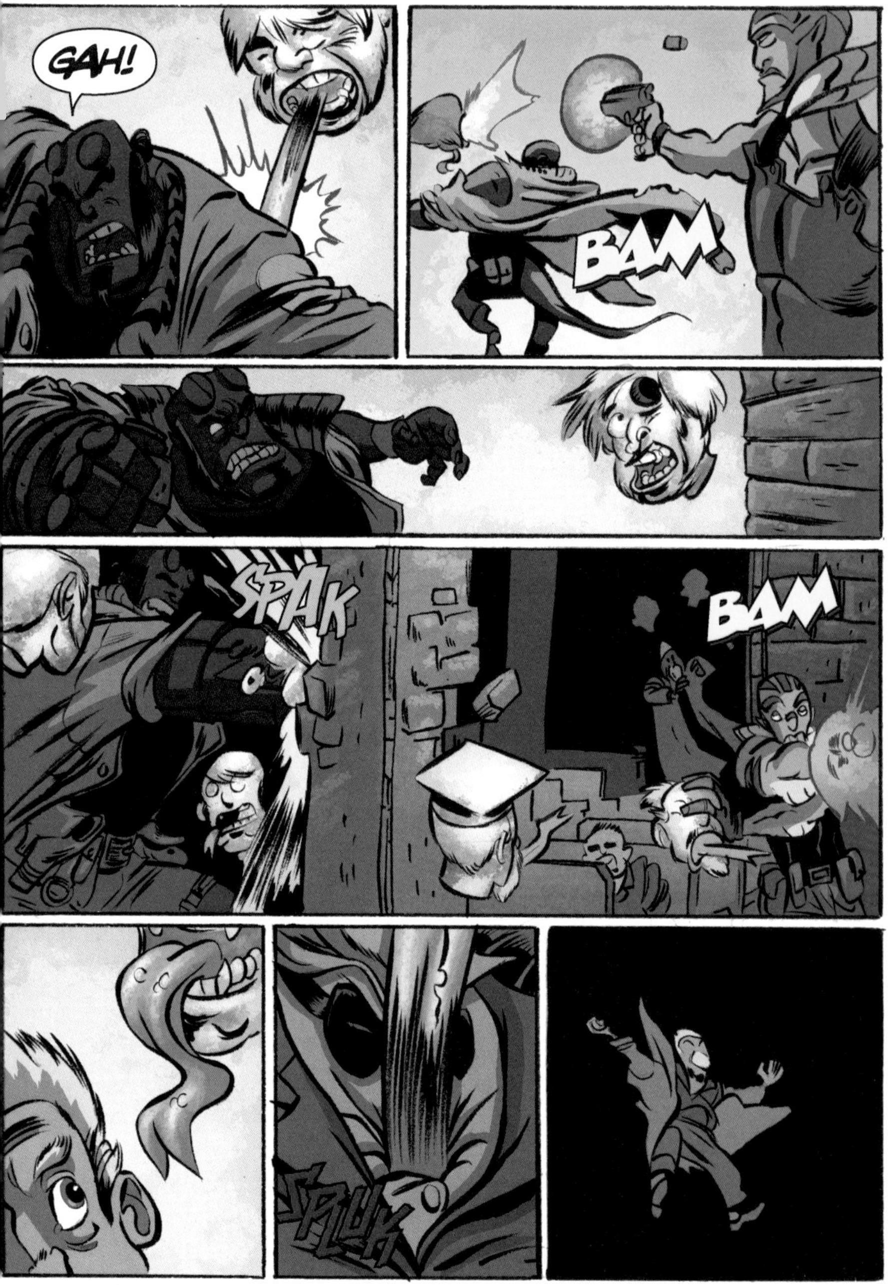
GAH!
BAM
SPAK
BAM
SPLUK

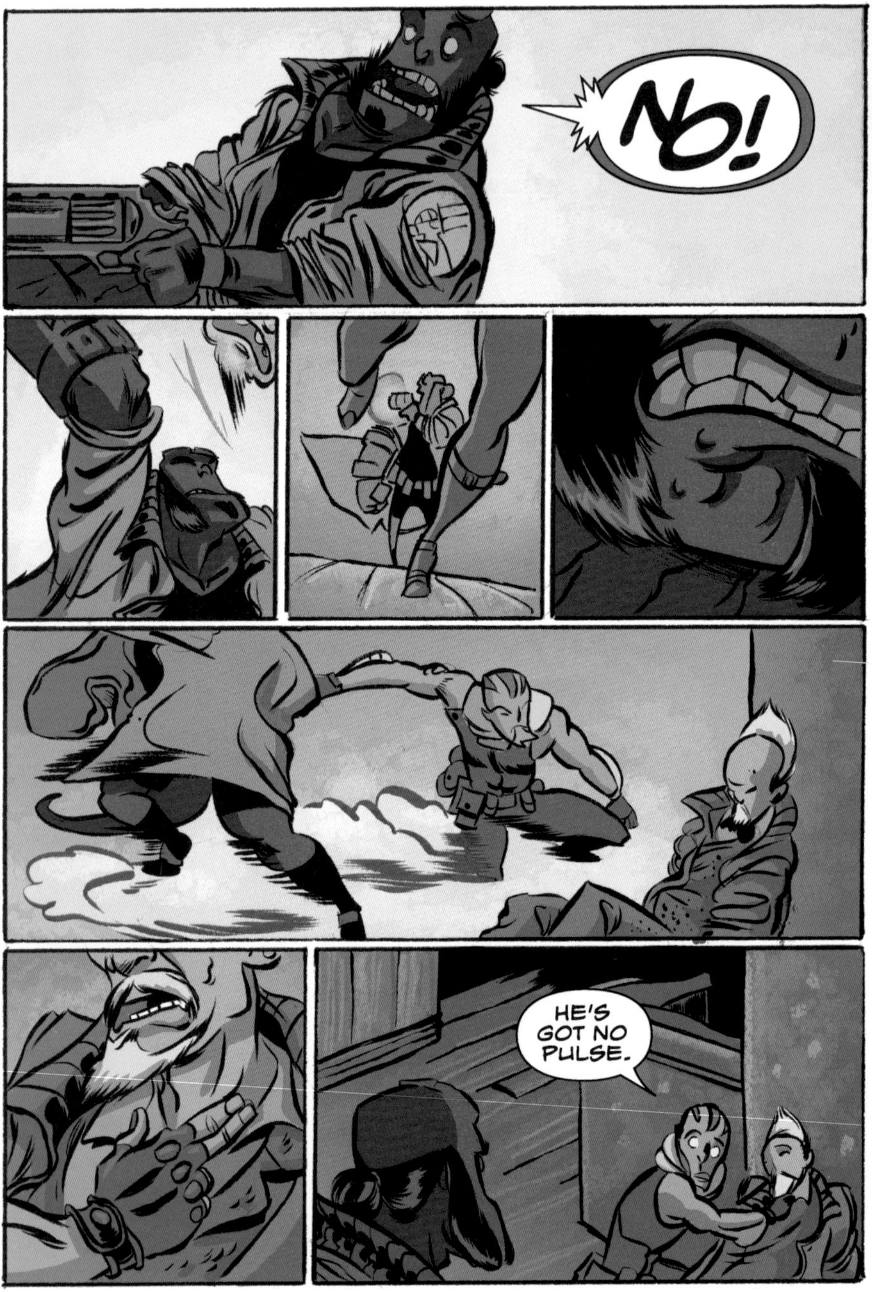
NO!
HE'S GOT NO PULSE.

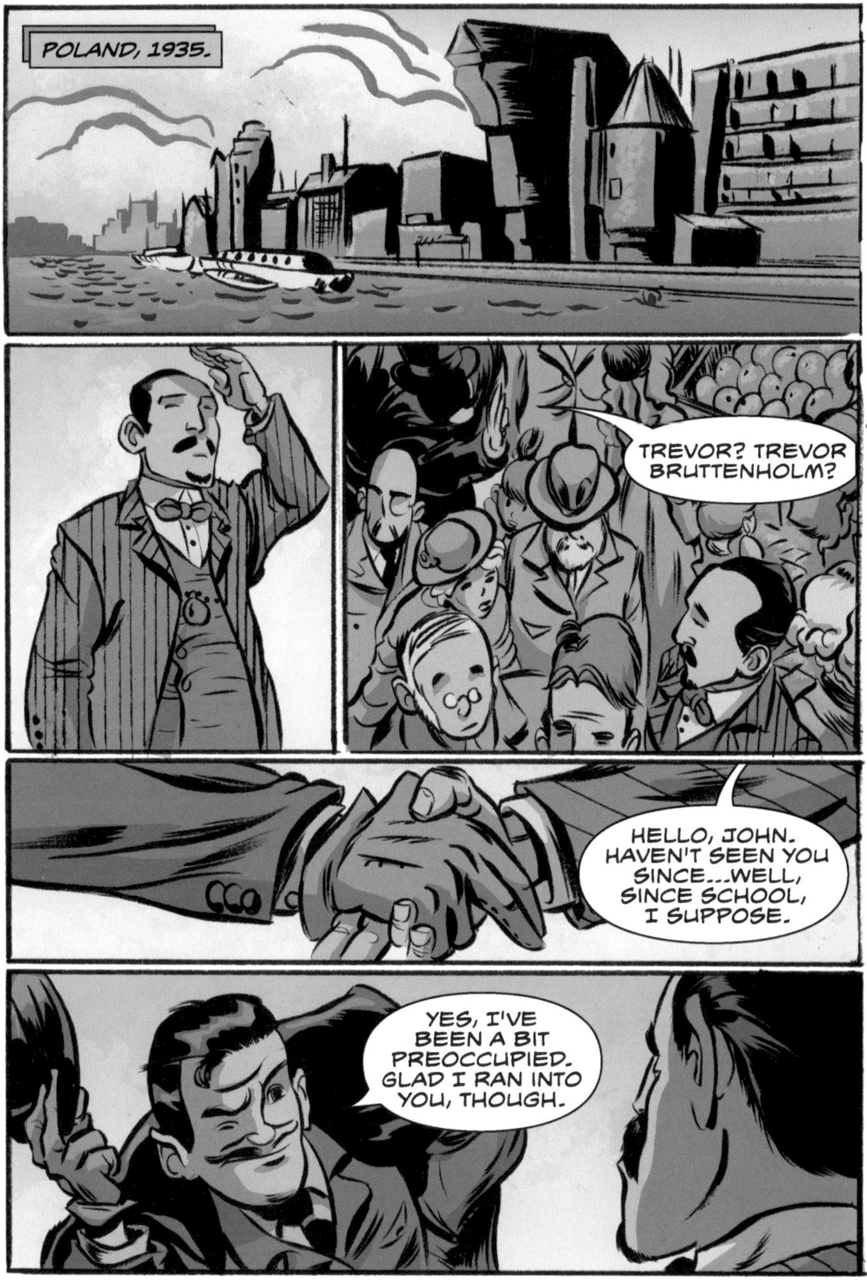
POLAND, 1935.
TREVOR? TREVOR BRUTTENHOLM?
HELLO, JOHN. HAVEN'T SEEN YOU SINCE...WELL, SINCE SCHOOL, I SUPPOSE.
YES, I'VE BEEN A BIT PREOCCUPIED. GLAD I RAN INTO YOU, THOUGH.

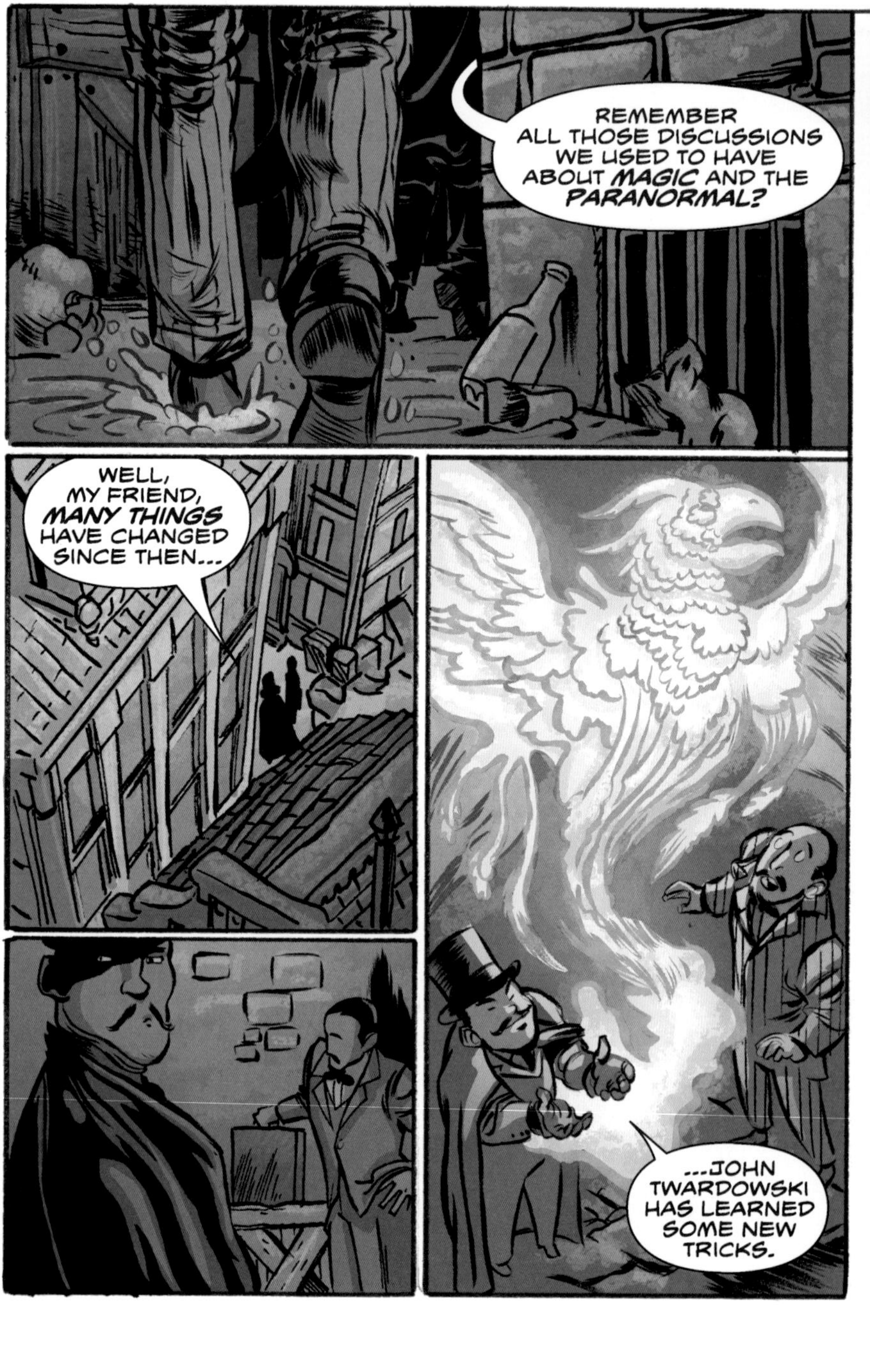

REMEMBER ALL THOSE DISCUSSIONS WE USED TO HAVE ABOUT *MAGIC* AND THE *PARANORMAL?*
WELL, MY FRIEND, *MANY THINGS* HAVE CHANGED SINCE THEN...
...JOHN TWARDOWSKI HAS LEARNED SOME NEW TRICKS.

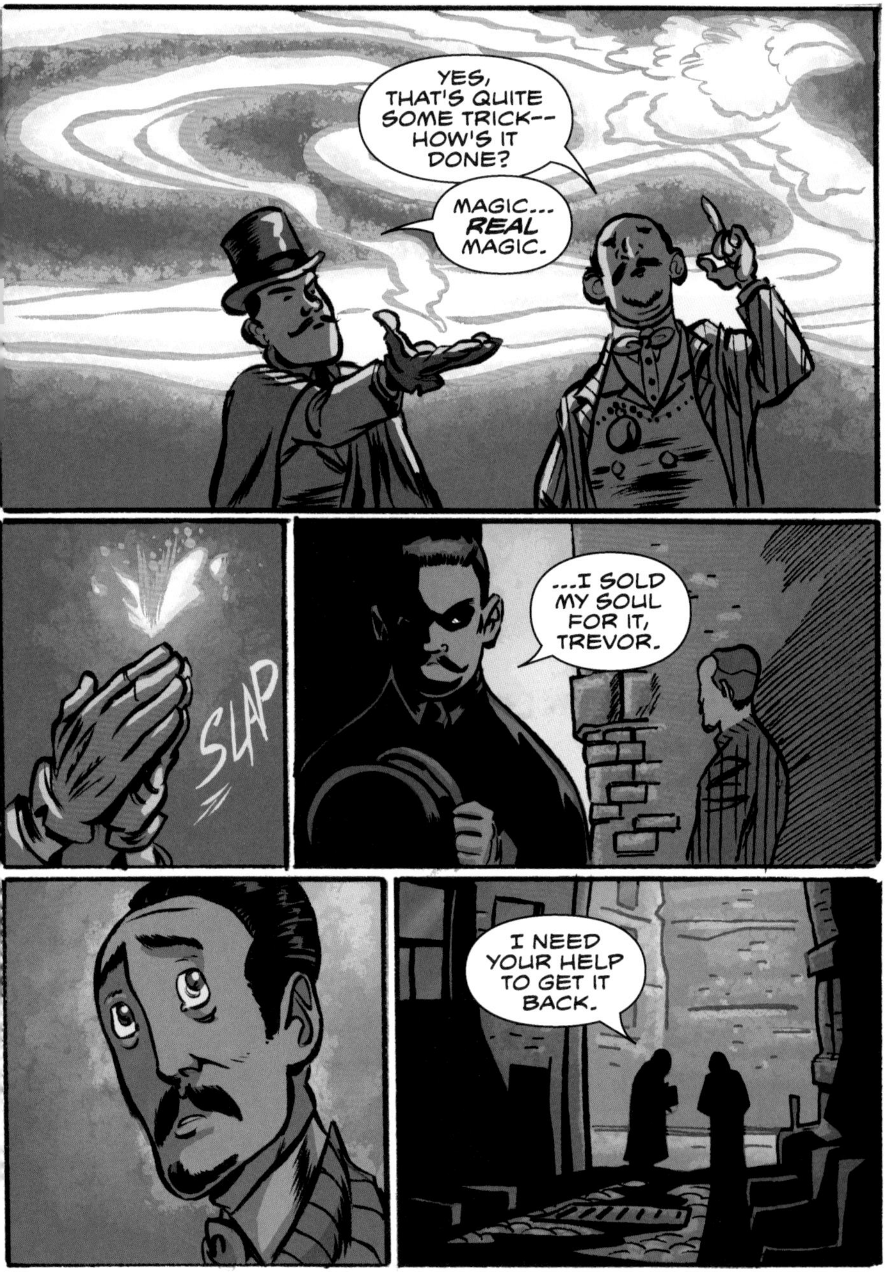
YES, THAT'S QUITE SOME TRICK-- HOW'S IT DONE?
MAGIC... REAL MAGIC.
SLAP
...I SOLD MY SOUL FOR IT, TREVOR.
I NEED YOUR HELP TO GET IT BACK.

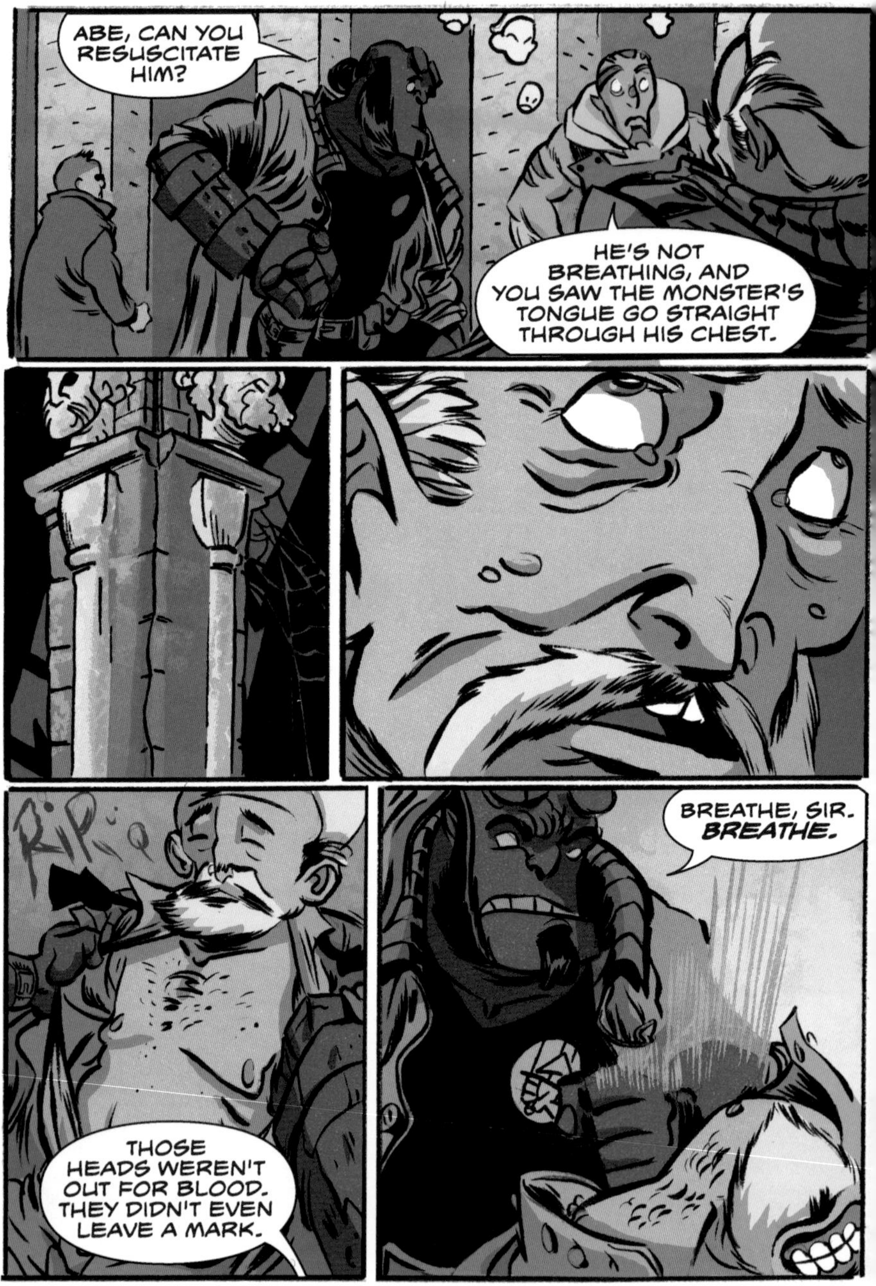
ABE, CAN YOU RESUSCITATE HIM?
HE'S NOT BREATHING, AND YOU SAW THE MONSTER'S TONGUE GO STRAIGHT THROUGH HIS CHEST.
RIP
THOSE HEADS WEREN'T OUT FOR BLOOD. THEY DIDN'T EVEN LEAVE A MARK.
BREATHE, SIR. *BREATHE.*

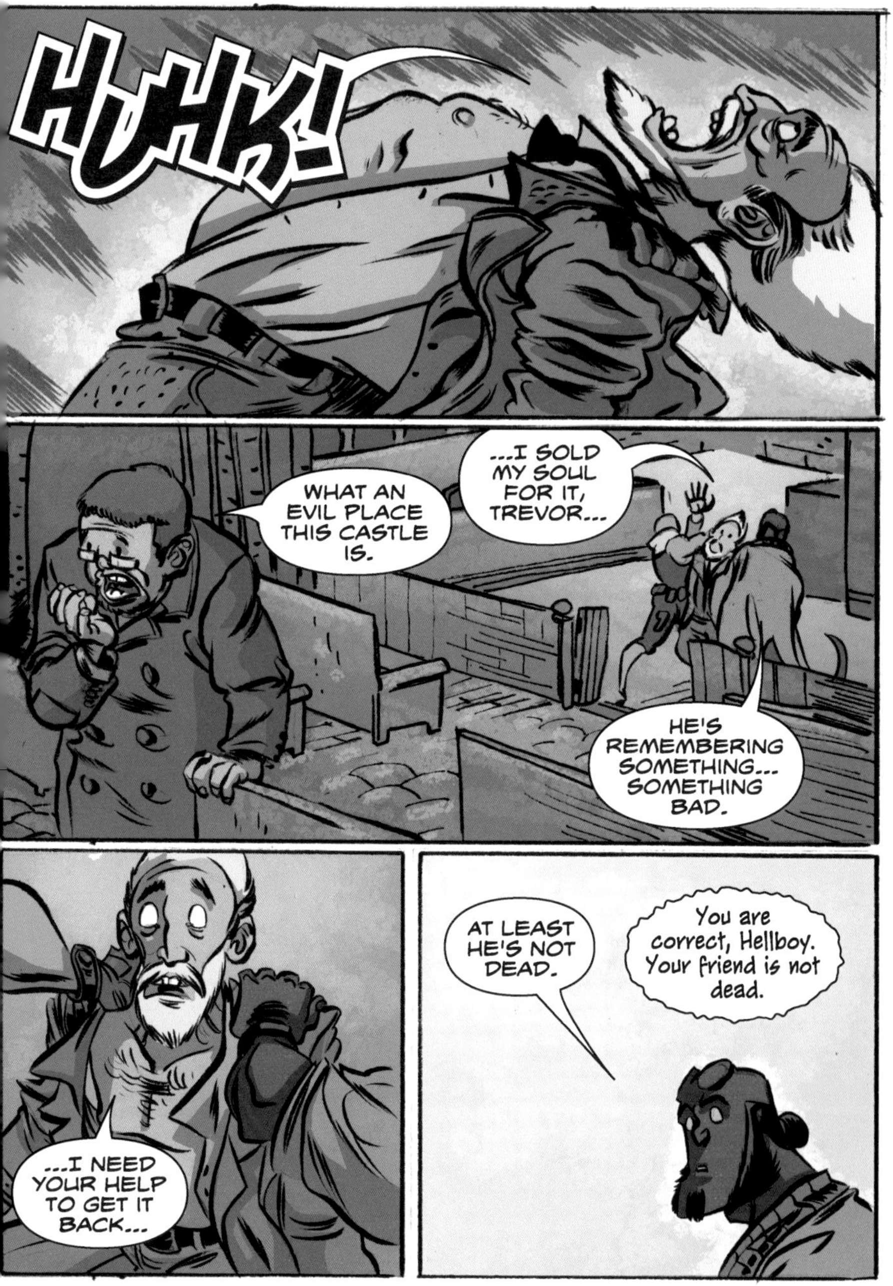
HUHK!
WHAT AN EVIL PLACE THIS CASTLE IS.
...I SOLD MY SOUL FOR IT, TREVOR...
HE'S REMEMBERING SOMETHING... SOMETHING BAD.
...I NEED YOUR HELP TO GET IT BACK...
AT LEAST HE'S NOT DEAD.
You are correct, Hellboy. Your friend is not dead.

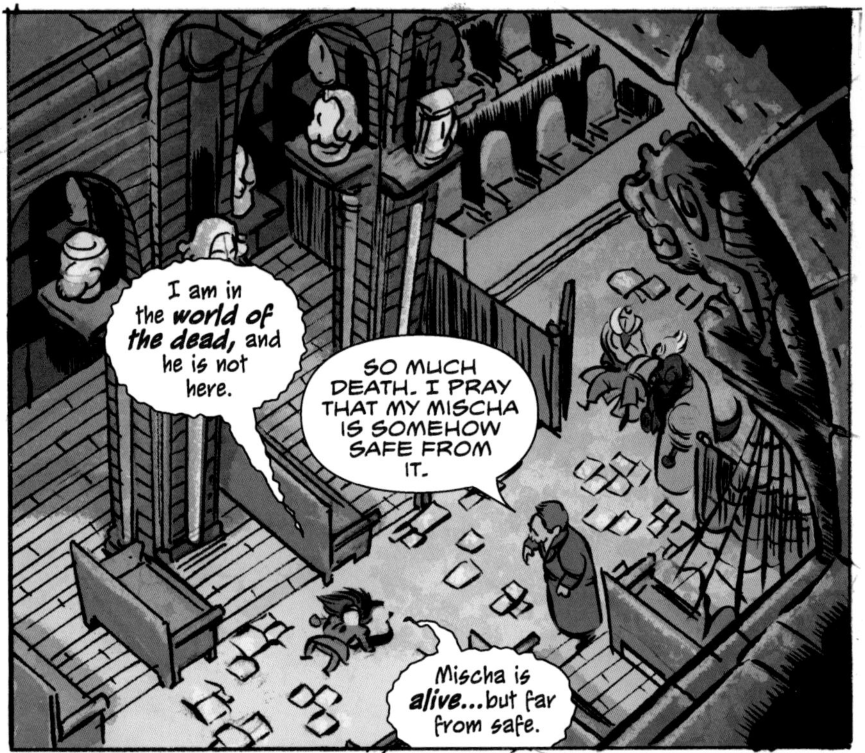
I am in the *world of the dead,* and he is not here.
SO MUCH DEATH. I PRAY THAT MY MISCHA IS SOMEHOW SAFE FROM IT.
Mischa is *alive...* but far from safe.

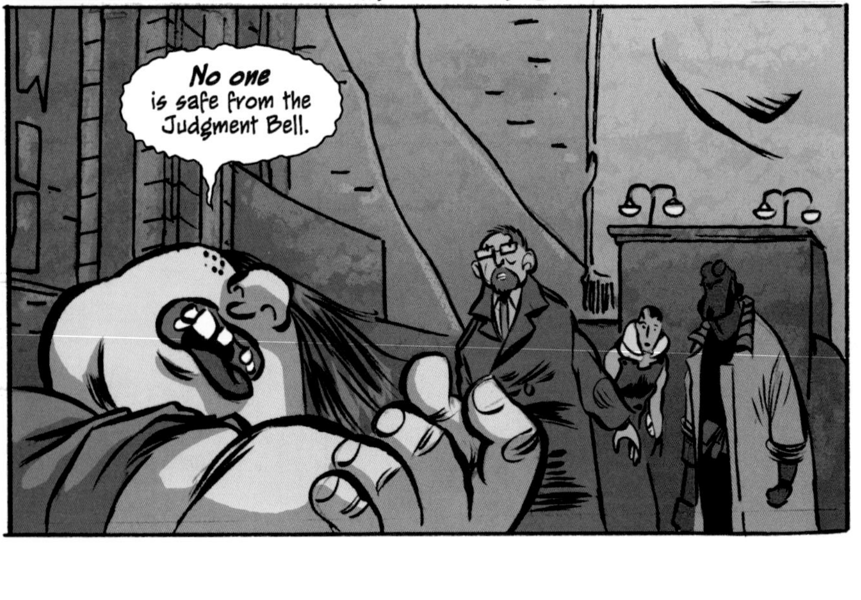
No one is safe from the Judgment Bell.

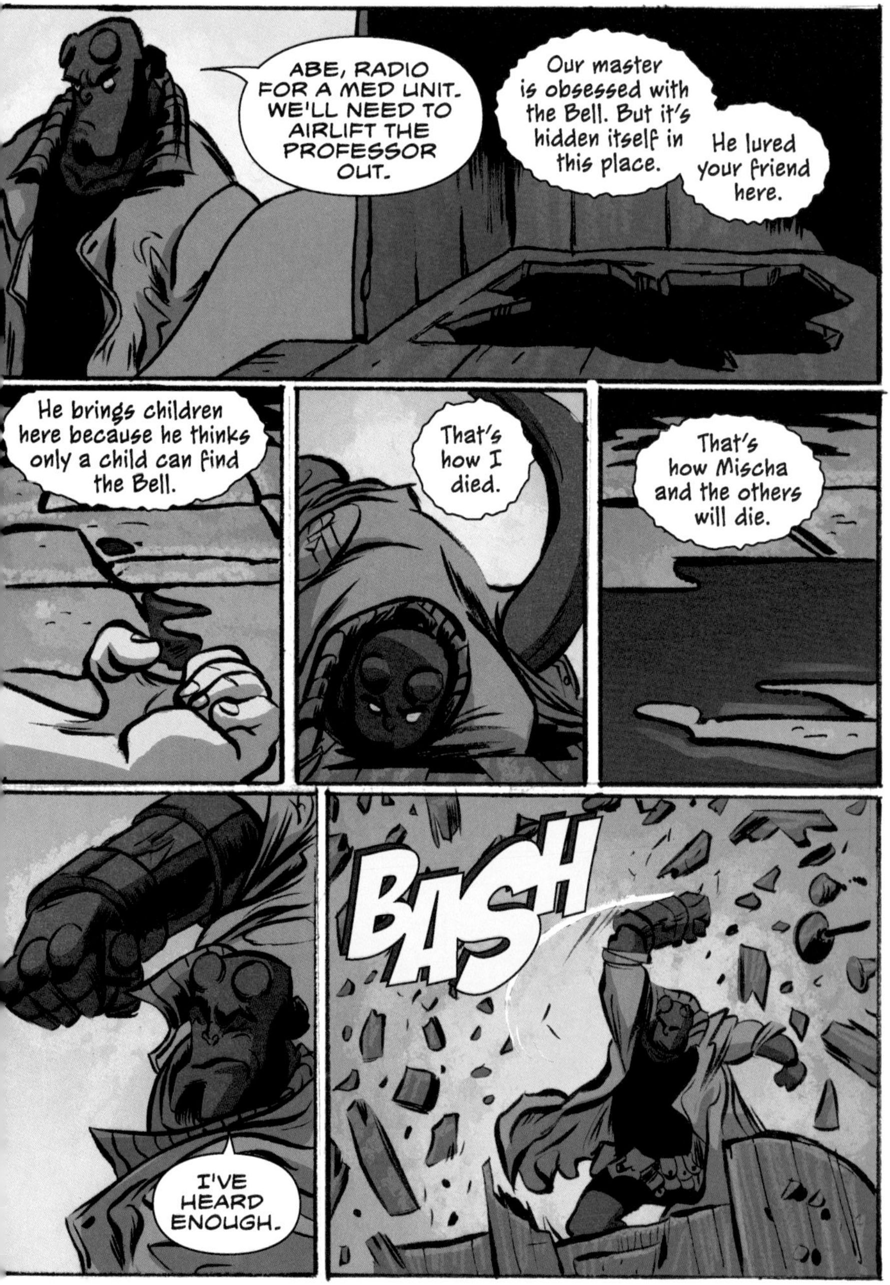
ABE, RADIO FOR A MED UNIT. WE'LL NEED TO AIRLIFT THE PROFESSOR OUT.
Our master is obsessed with the Bell. But it's hidden itself in this place.
He lured your friend here.
He brings children here because he thinks only a child can find the Bell.
That's how I died.
That's how Mischa and the others will die.
I'VE HEARD ENOUGH.
BASH

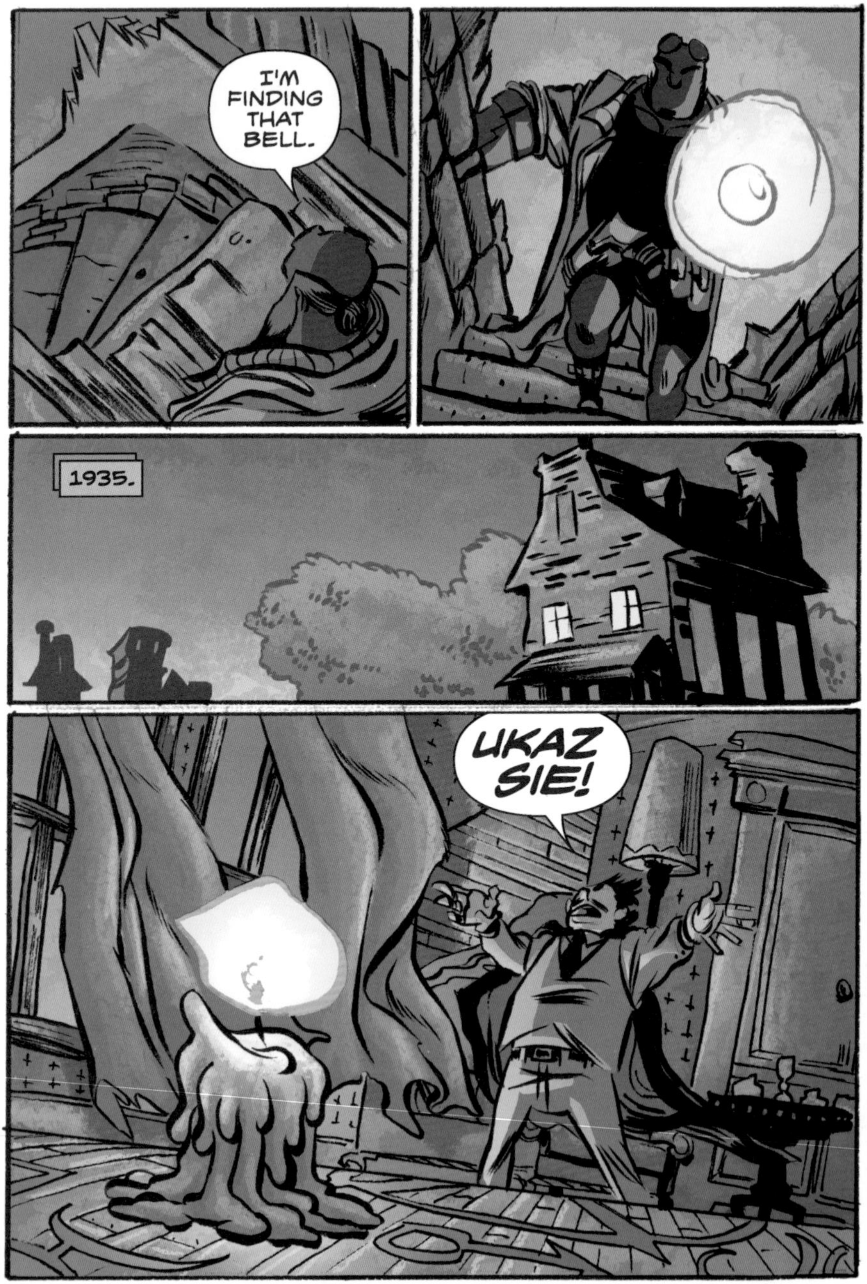
I'M FINDING THAT BELL.
1935.
UKAZ SIE!

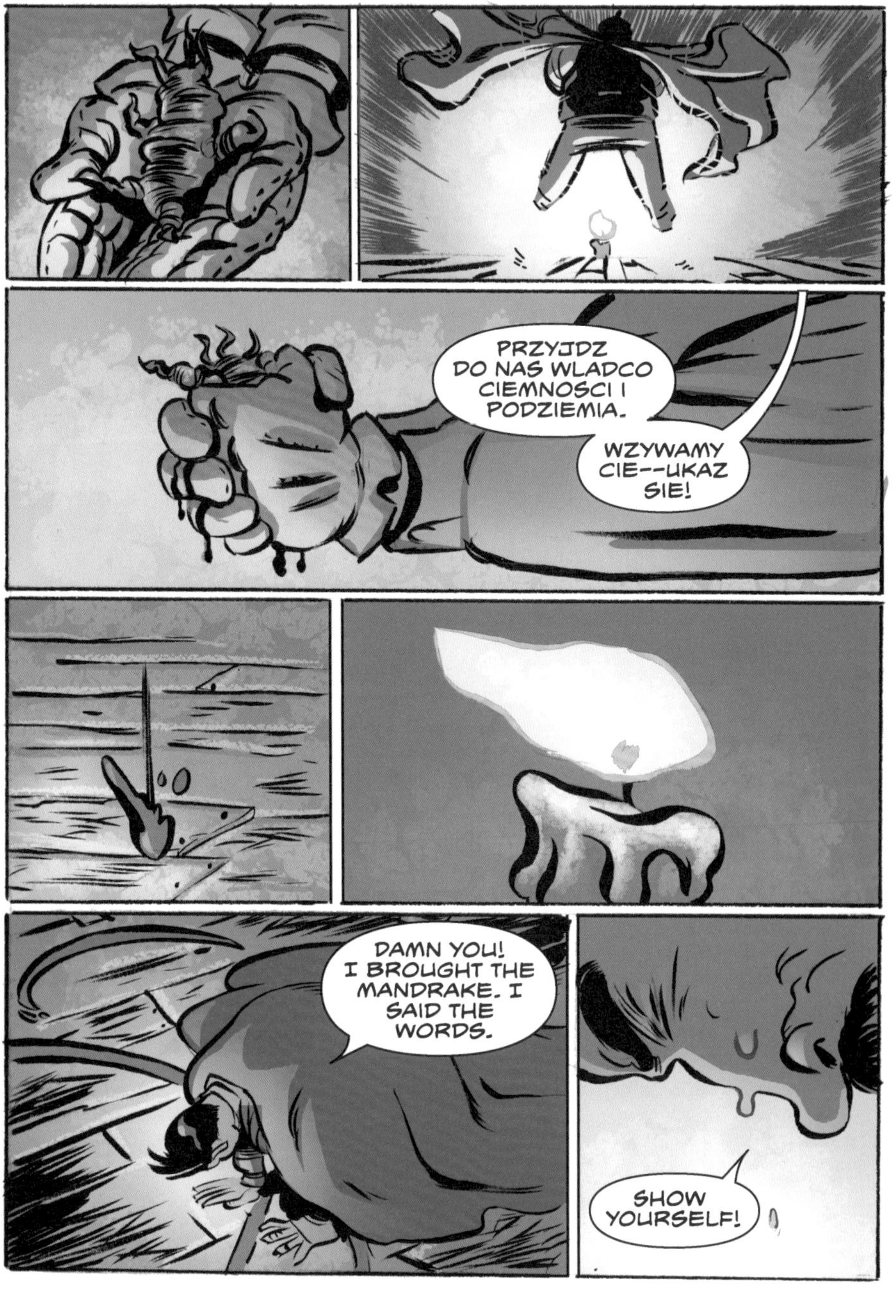
PRZYJDZ DO NAS WLADCO CIEMNOSCI I PODZIEMIA.
WZYWAMY CIE--UKAZ SIE!
DAMN YOU! I BROUGHT THE MANDRAKE. I SAID THE WORDS.
SHOW YOURSELF!

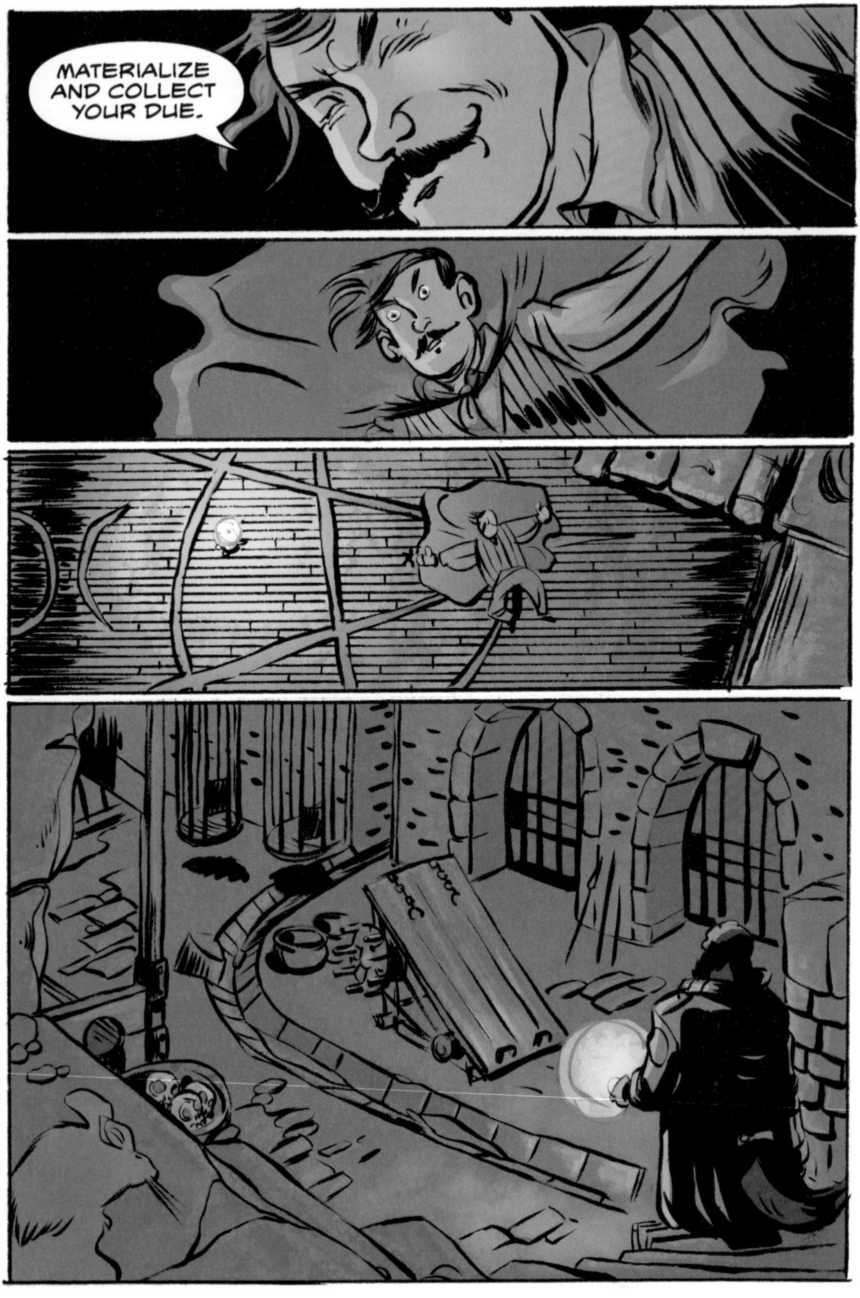
MATERIALIZE AND COLLECT YOUR DUE.

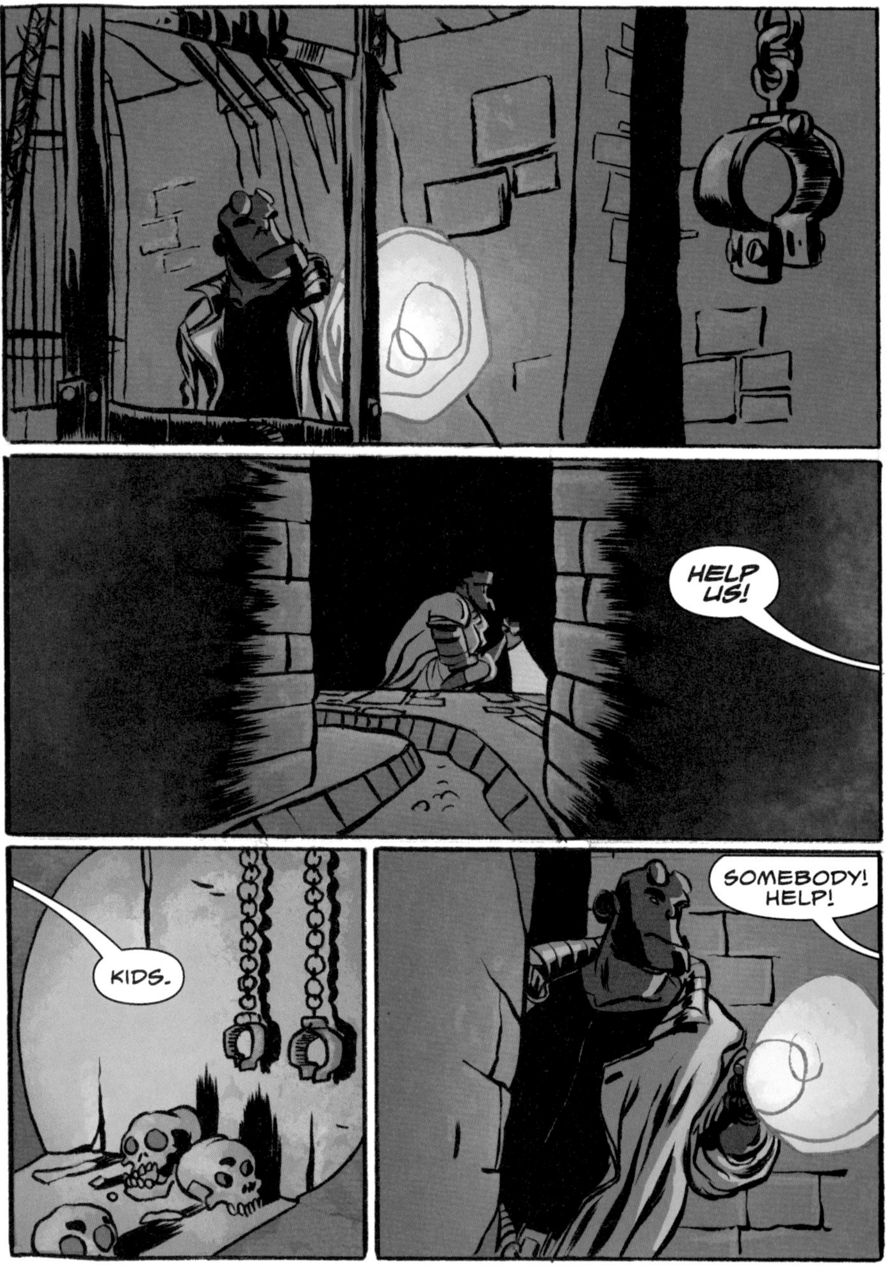
HELP US!
KIDS.
SOMEBODY! HELP!

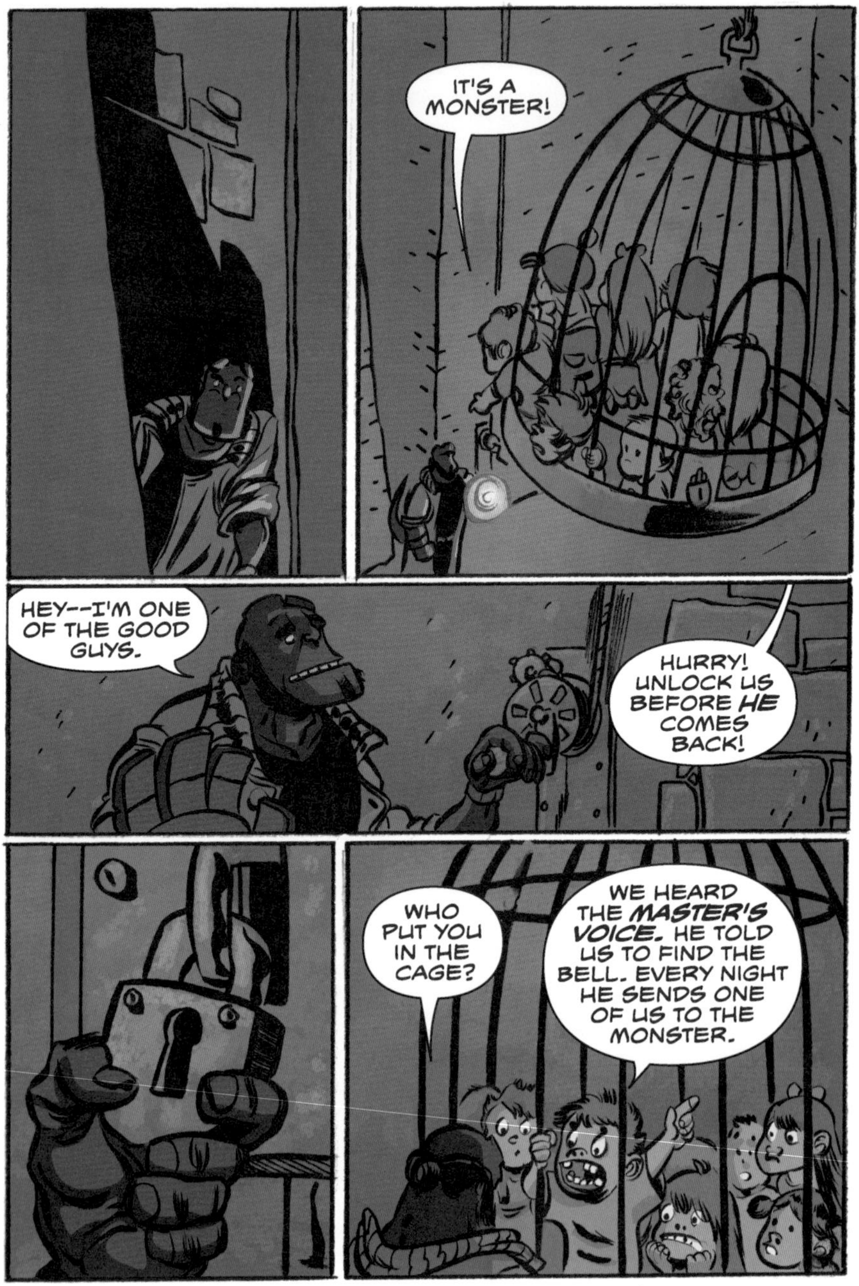

IT'S A MONSTER!
HEY--I'M ONE OF THE GOOD GUYS.
HURRY! UNLOCK US BEFORE *HE* COMES BACK!
WHO PUT YOU IN THE CAGE?
WE HEARD THE ***MASTER'S VOICE.*** HE TOLD US TO FIND THE BELL. EVERY NIGHT HE SENDS ONE OF US TO THE MONSTER.

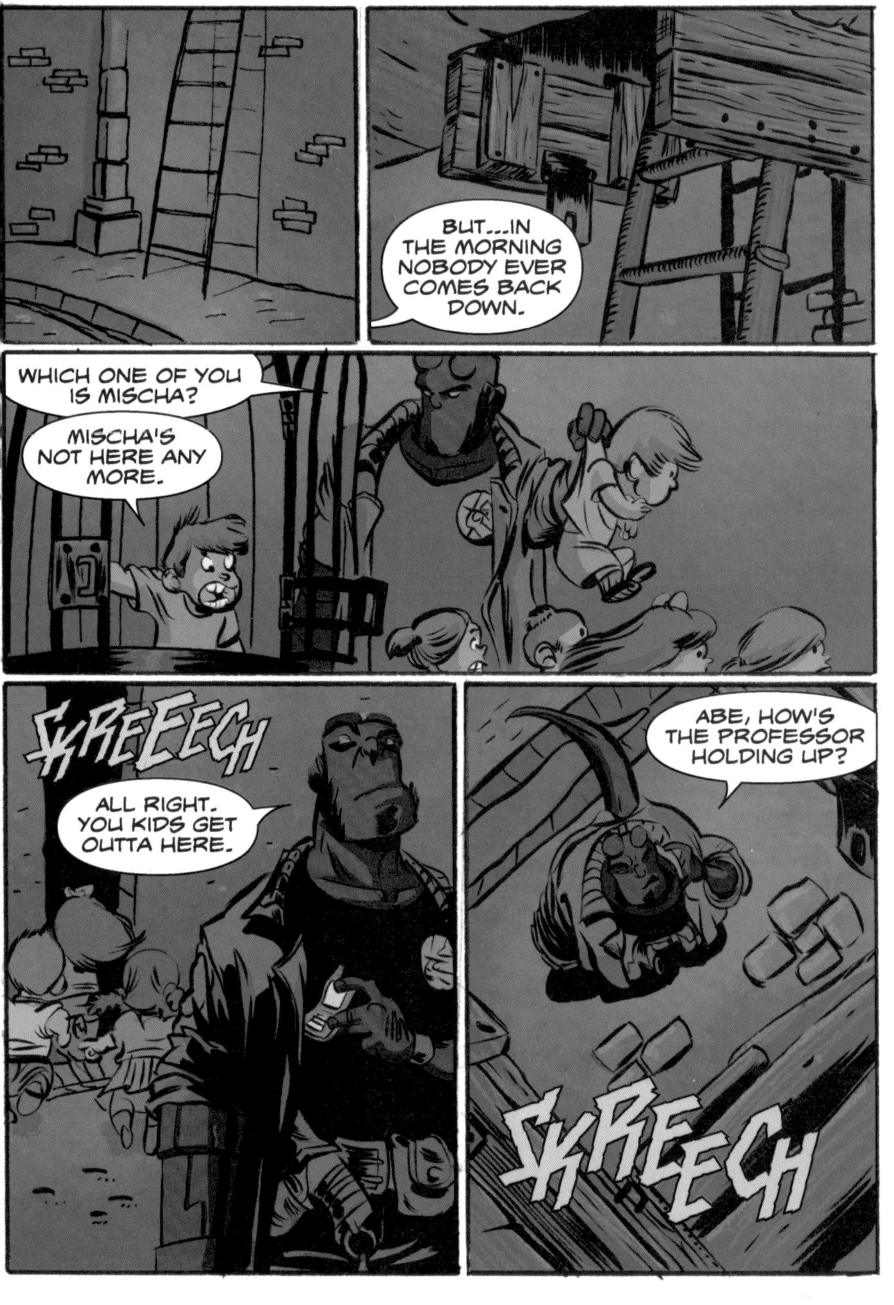
BUT...IN THE MORNING NOBODY EVER COMES BACK DOWN.
WHICH ONE OF YOU IS MISCHA?
MISCHA'S NOT HERE ANY MORE.
SKREEECH
ALL RIGHT. YOU KIDS GET OUTTA HERE.
ABE, HOW'S THE PROFESSOR HOLDING UP?
SKREECH

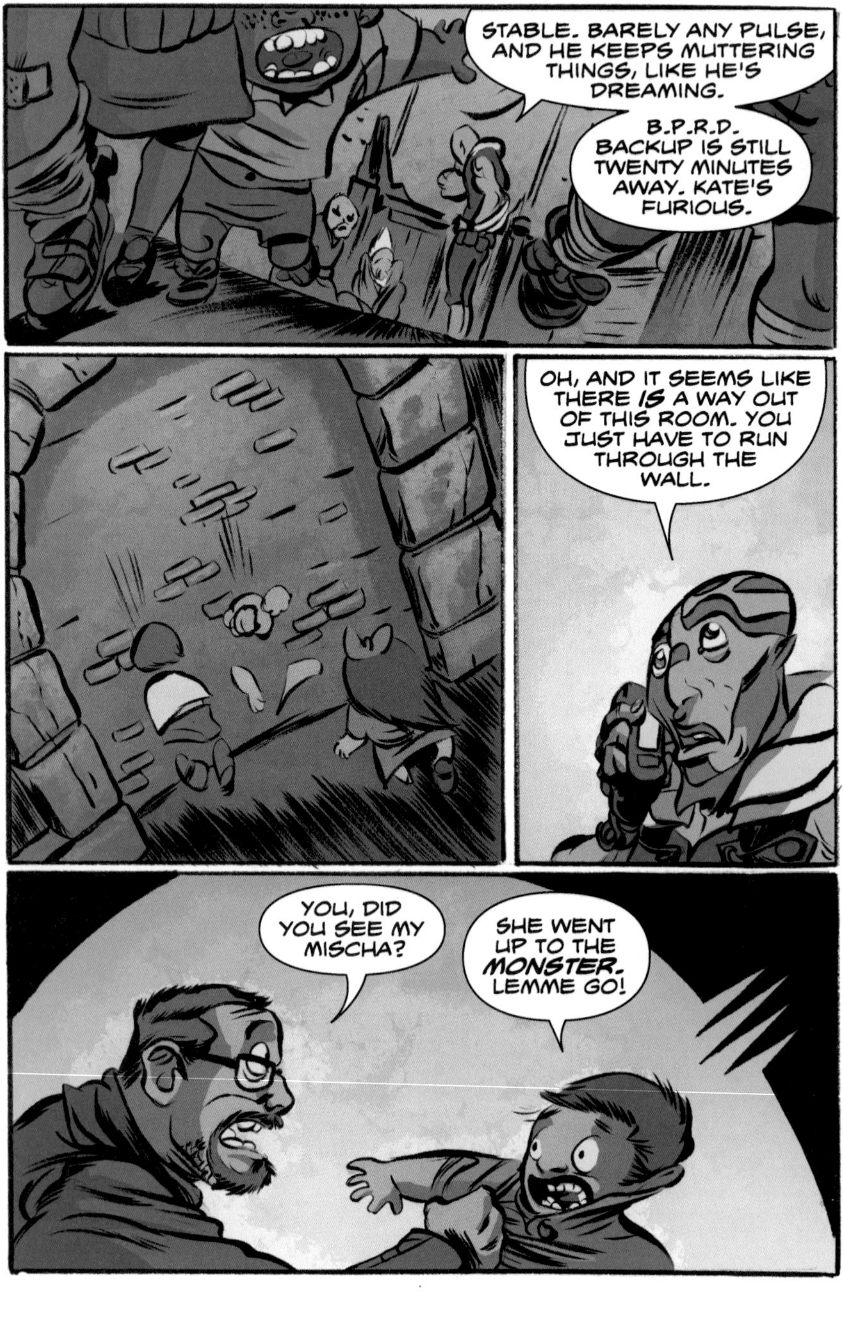
STABLE. BARELY ANY PULSE, AND HE KEEPS MUTTERING THINGS, LIKE HE'S DREAMING.
B.P.R.D. BACKUP IS STILL TWENTY MINUTES AWAY. KATE'S FURIOUS.
OH, AND IT SEEMS LIKE THERE *IS* A WAY OUT OF THIS ROOM. YOU JUST HAVE TO RUN THROUGH THE WALL.
YOU, DID YOU SEE MY MISCHA?
SHE WENT UP TO THE ***MONSTER.*** LEMME GO!

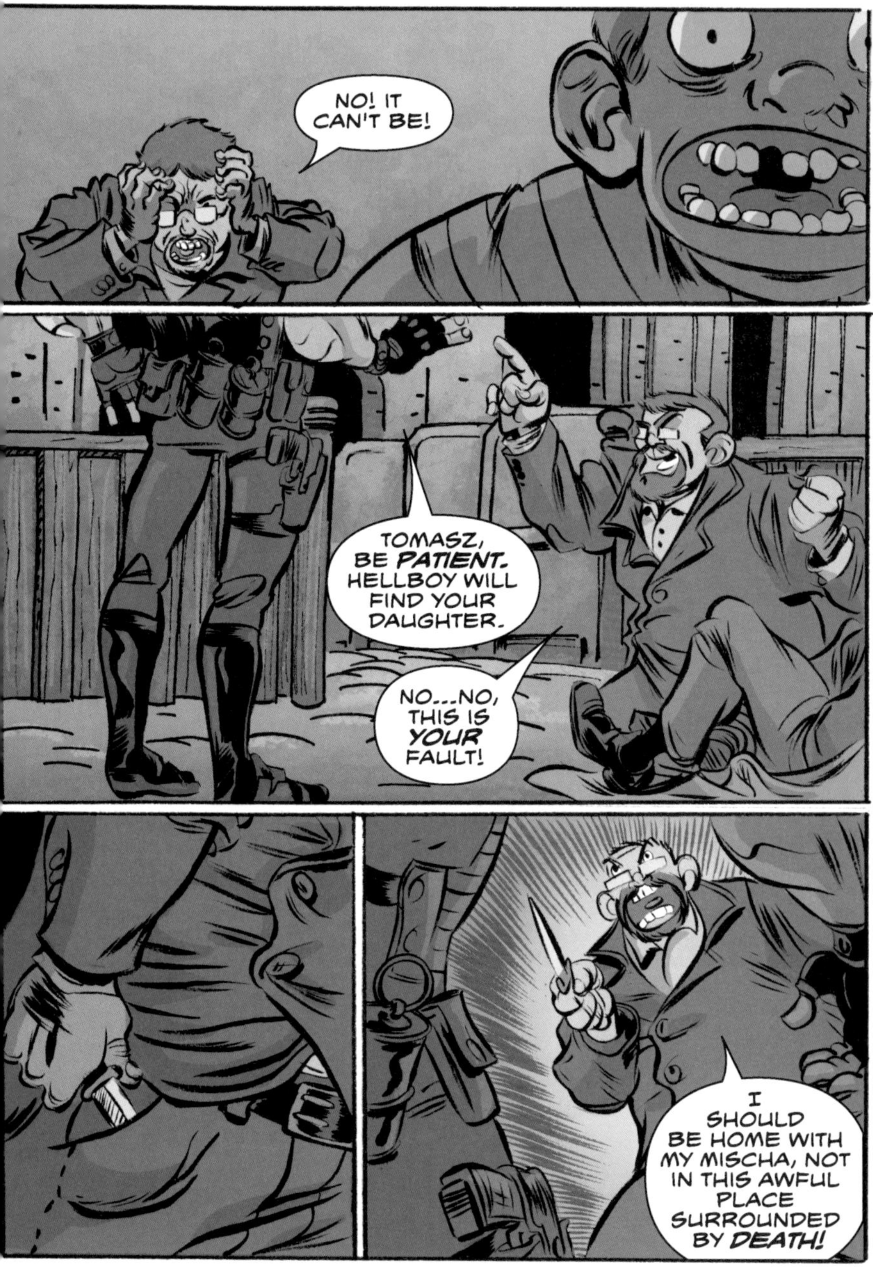
NO! IT CAN'T BE!
TOMASZ, BE *PATIENT*. HELLBOY WILL FIND YOUR DAUGHTER.
NO...NO, THIS IS *YOUR* FAULT!
I SHOULD BE HOME WITH MY MISCHA, NOT IN THIS AWFUL PLACE SURROUNDED BY *DEATH!*

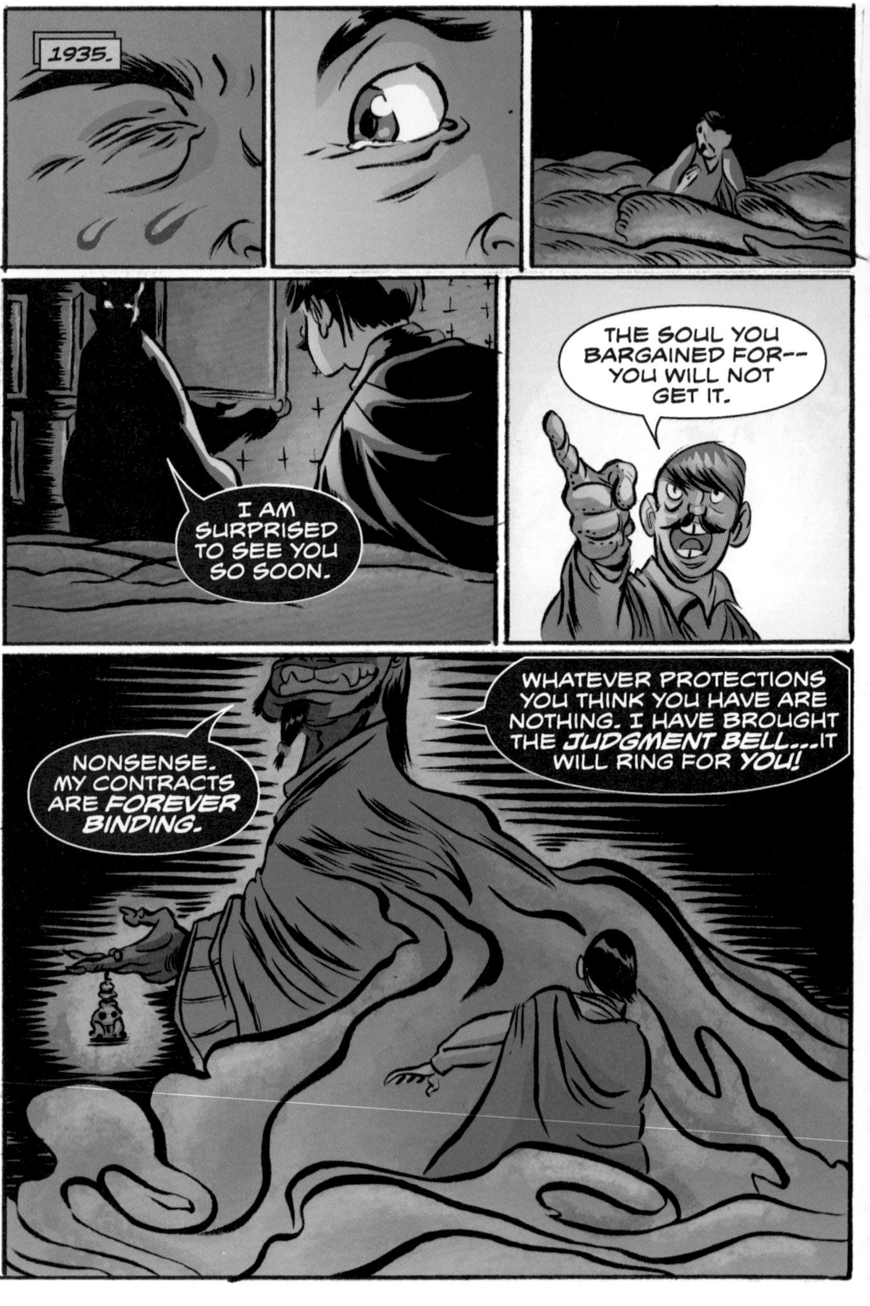
1935.
I AM SURPRISED TO SEE YOU SO SOON.
THE SOUL YOU BARGAINED FOR-- YOU WILL NOT GET IT.
NONSENSE. MY CONTRACTS ARE *FOREVER BINDING.*
WHATEVER PROTECTIONS YOU THINK YOU HAVE ARE NOTHING. I HAVE BROUGHT THE *JUDGMENT BELL*...IT WILL RING FOR *YOU!*

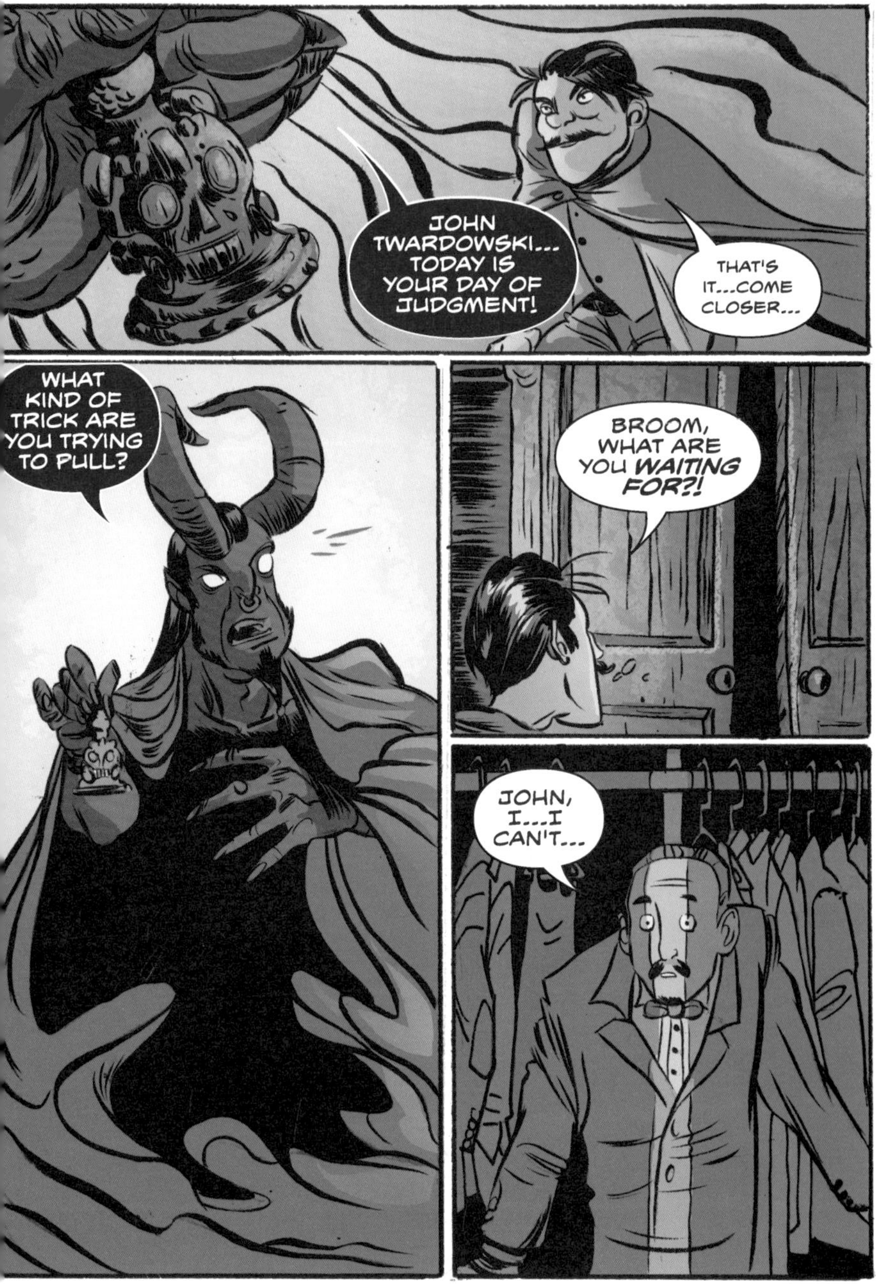
JOHN TWARDOWSKI... TODAY IS YOUR DAY OF JUDGMENT!
THAT'S IT...COME CLOSER...
WHAT KIND OF TRICK ARE YOU TRYING TO PULL?
BROOM, WHAT ARE YOU *WAITING FOR?!*
JOHN, I...I CAN'T...

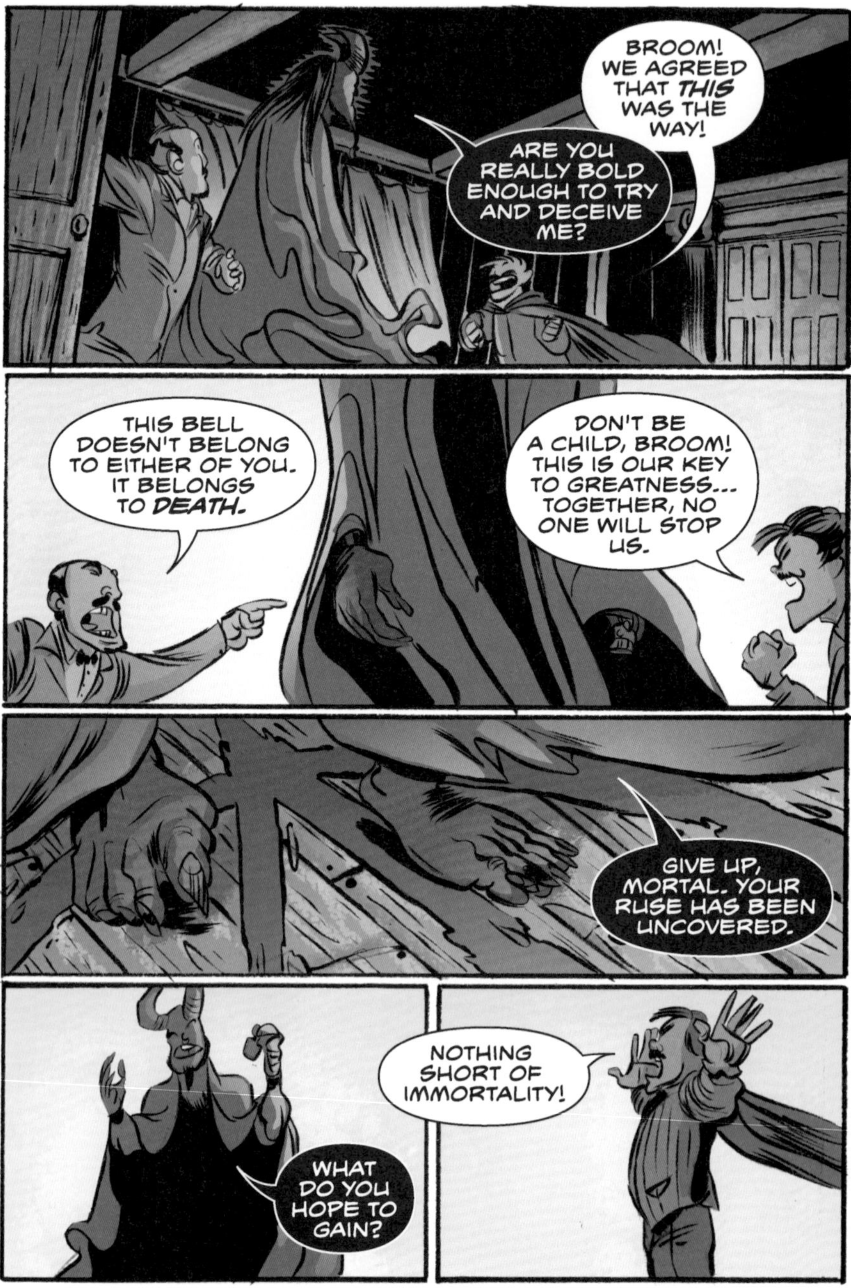
BROOM! WE AGREED THAT THIS WAS THE WAY!
ARE YOU REALLY BOLD ENOUGH TO TRY AND DECEIVE ME?
THIS BELL DOESN'T BELONG TO EITHER OF YOU. IT BELONGS TO DEATH.
DON'T BE A CHILD, BROOM! THIS IS OUR KEY TO GREATNESS... TOGETHER, NO ONE WILL STOP US.
GIVE UP, MORTAL. YOUR RUSE HAS BEEN UNCOVERED.
WHAT DO YOU HOPE TO GAIN?
NOTHING SHORT OF IMMORTALITY!

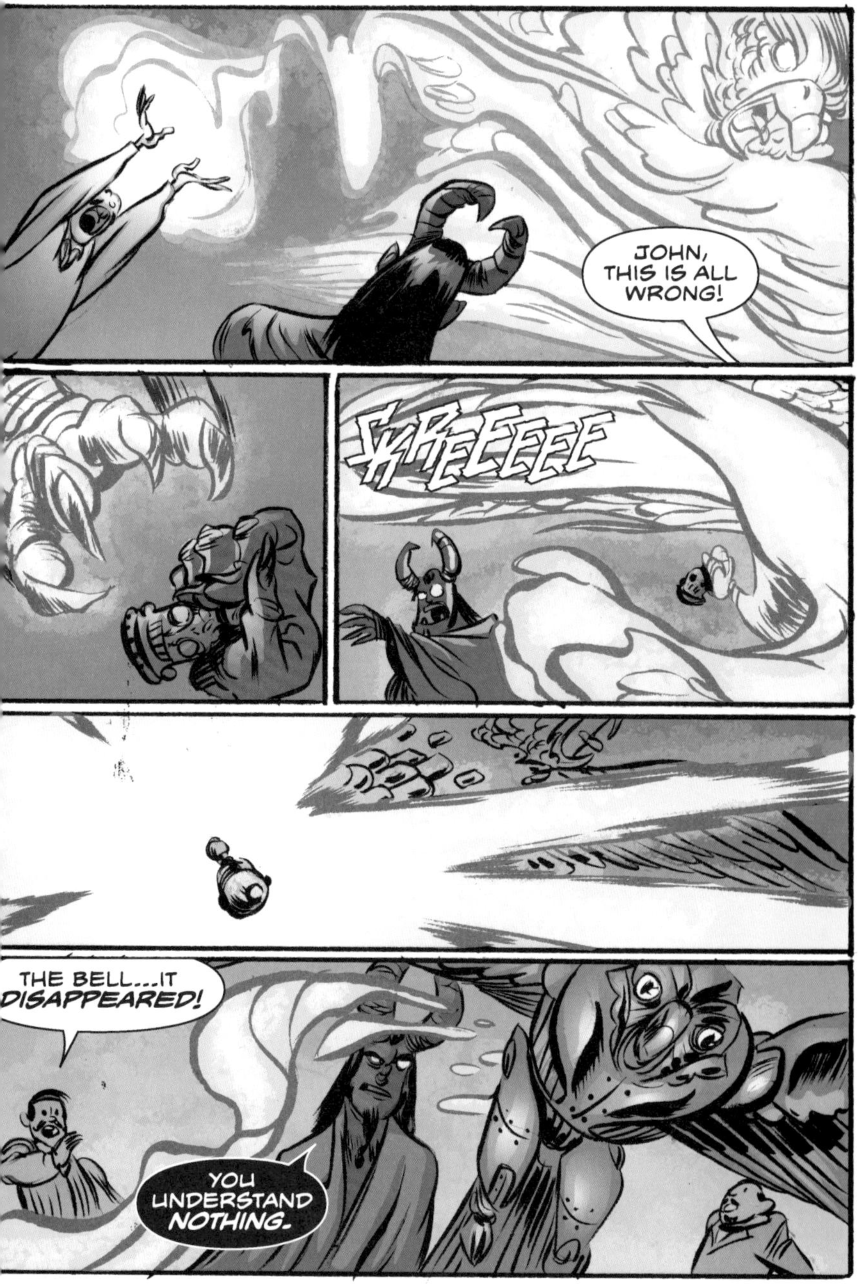
JOHN, THIS IS ALL WRONG!
SKREEEEEE
THE BELL...IT DISAPPEARED!
YOU UNDERSTAND NOTHING.

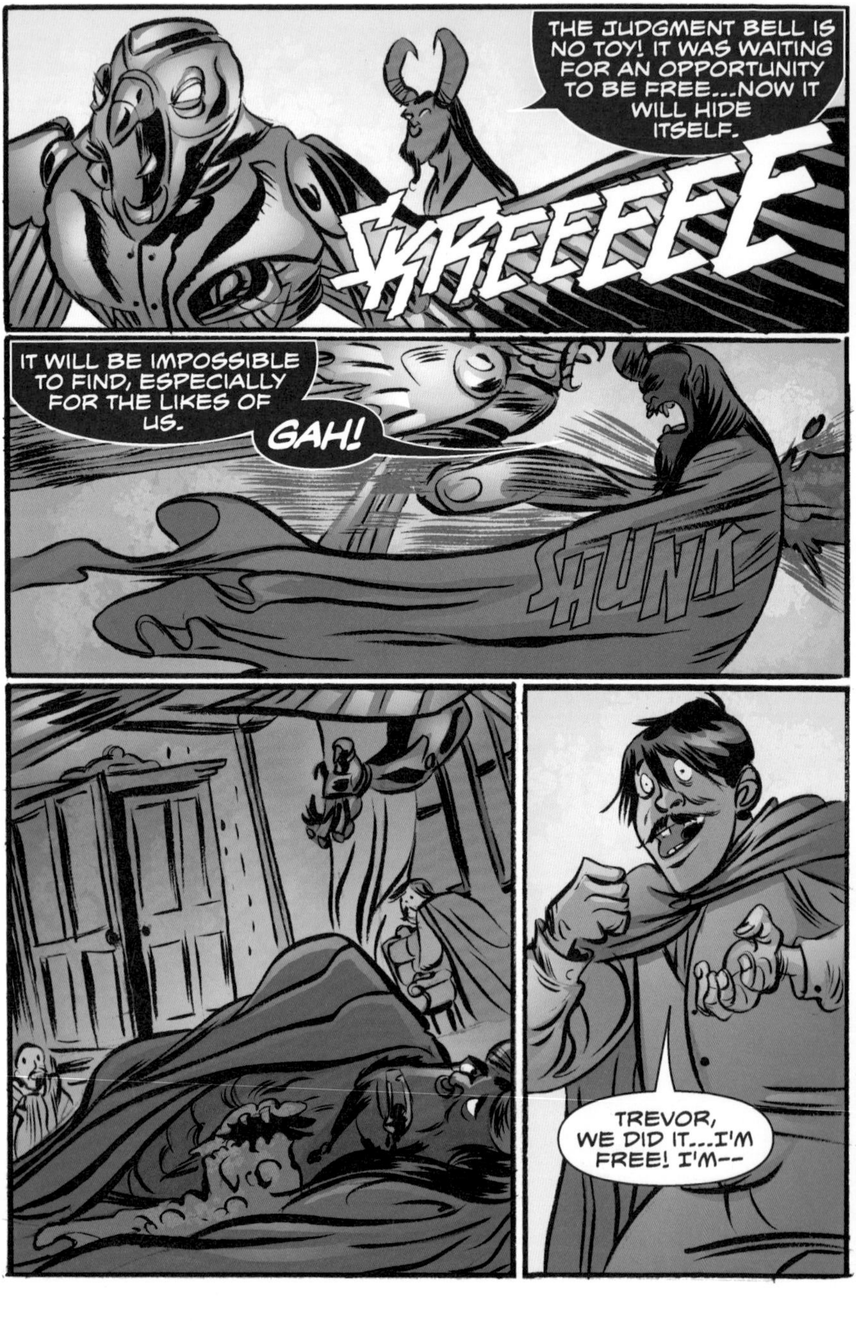
THE JUDGMENT BELL IS NO TOY! IT WAS WAITING FOR AN OPPORTUNITY TO BE FREE...NOW IT WILL HIDE ITSELF.
SKREEEEEE
IT WILL BE IMPOSSIBLE TO FIND, ESPECIALLY FOR THE LIKES OF US.
GAH!
SHUNK
TREVOR, WE DID IT...I'M FREE! I'M--

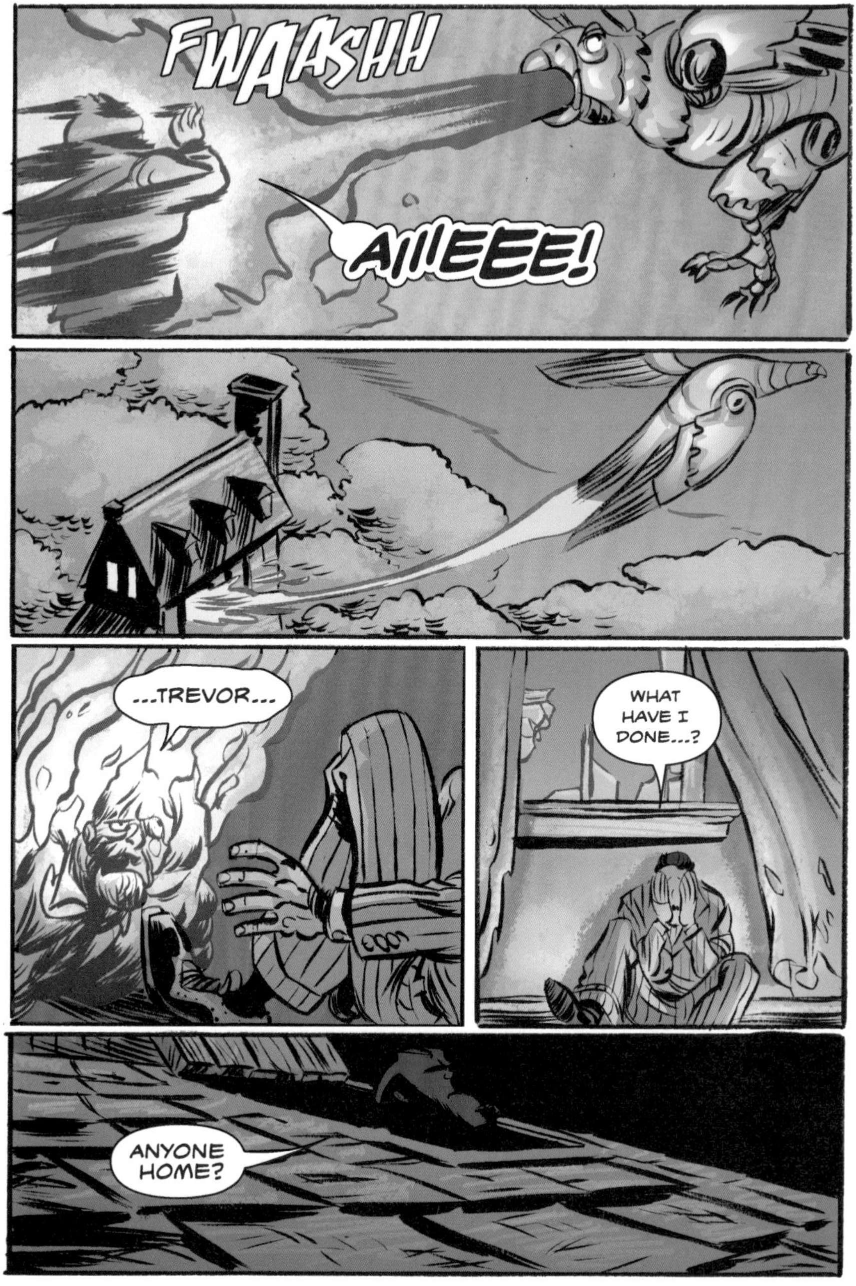
FWAASHH
AIIEEEE!
...TREVOR...
WHAT HAVE I DONE...?
ANYONE HOME?

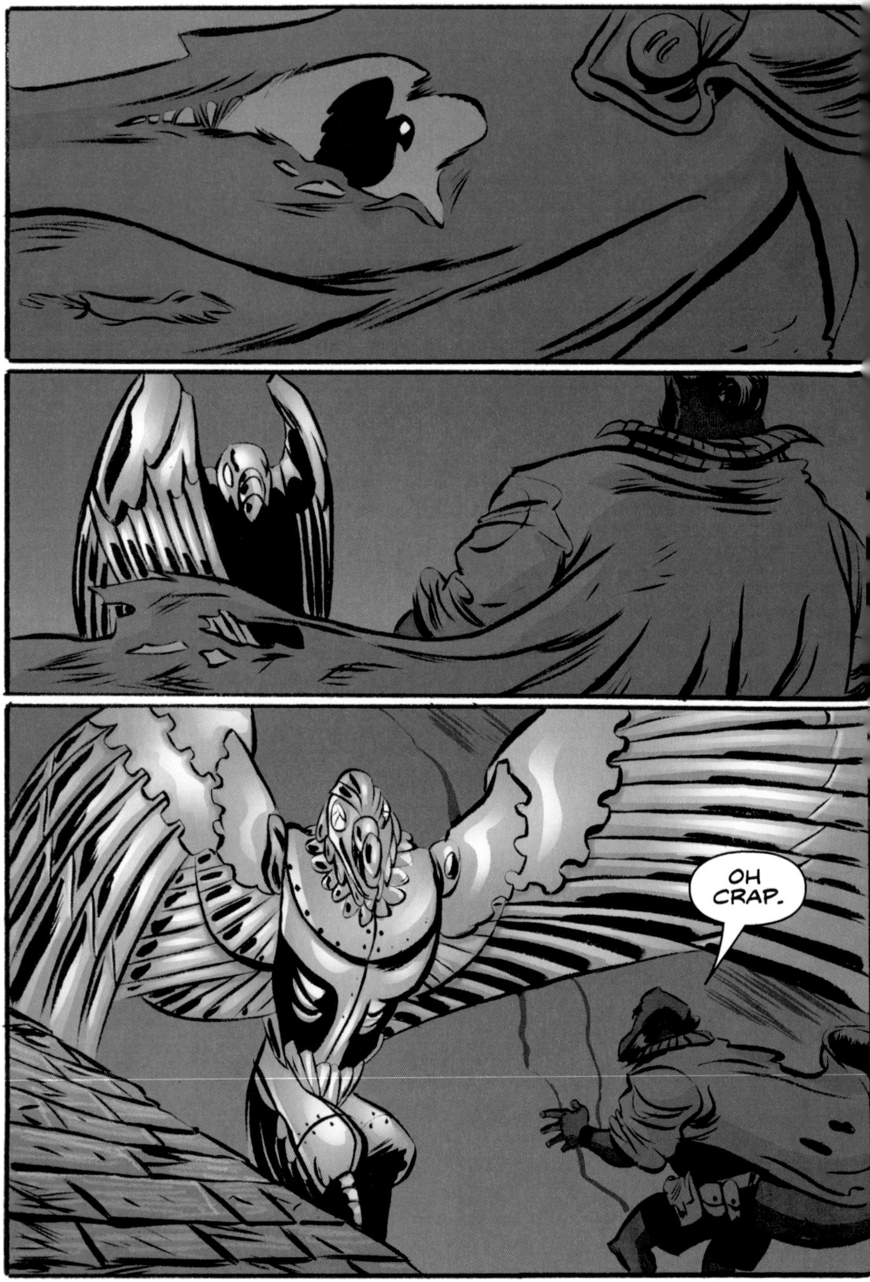
OH CRAP.

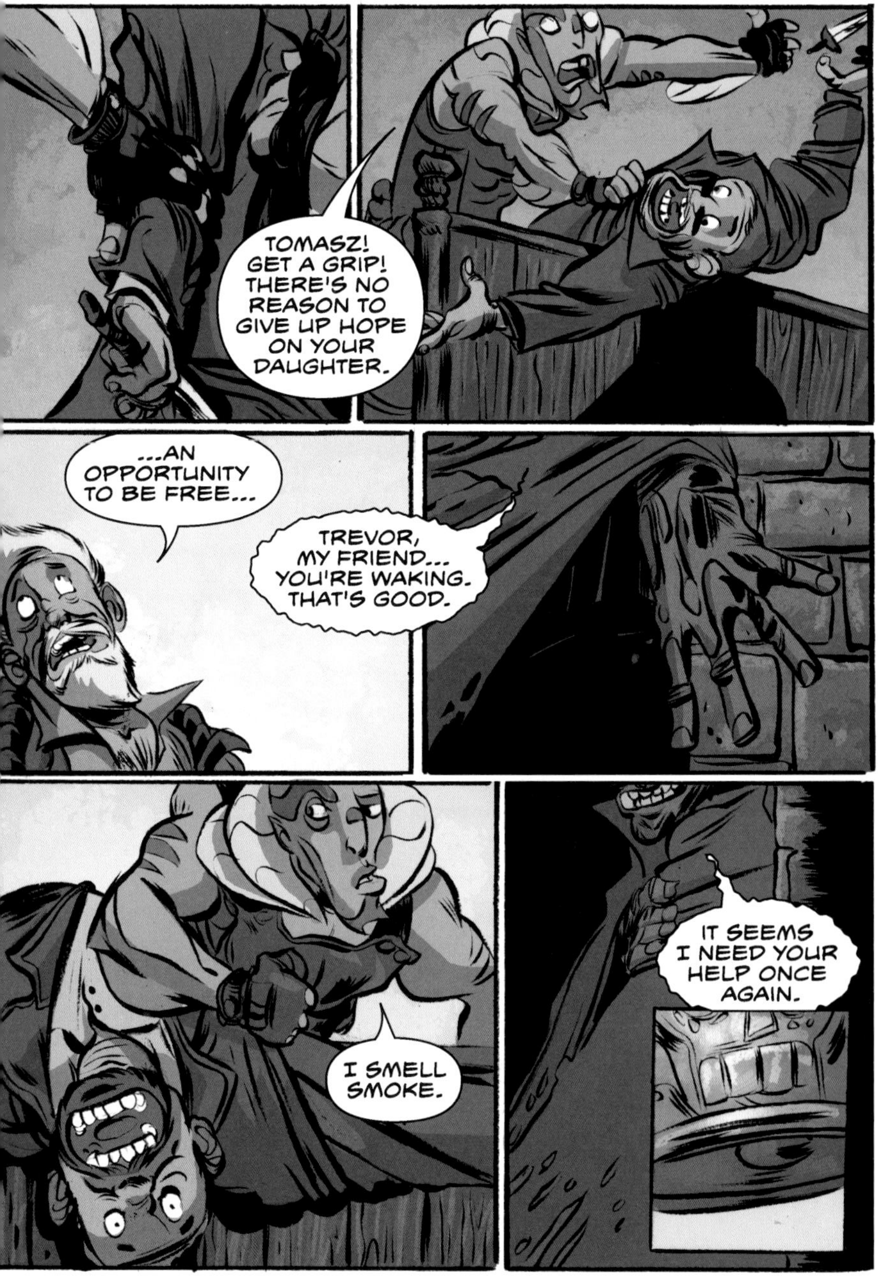
TOMASZ! GET A GRIP! THERE'S NO REASON TO GIVE UP HOPE ON YOUR DAUGHTER.
...AN OPPORTUNITY TO BE FREE...
TREVOR, MY FRIEND... YOU'RE WAKING. THAT'S GOOD.
I SMELL SMOKE.
IT SEEMS I NEED YOUR HELP ONCE AGAIN.

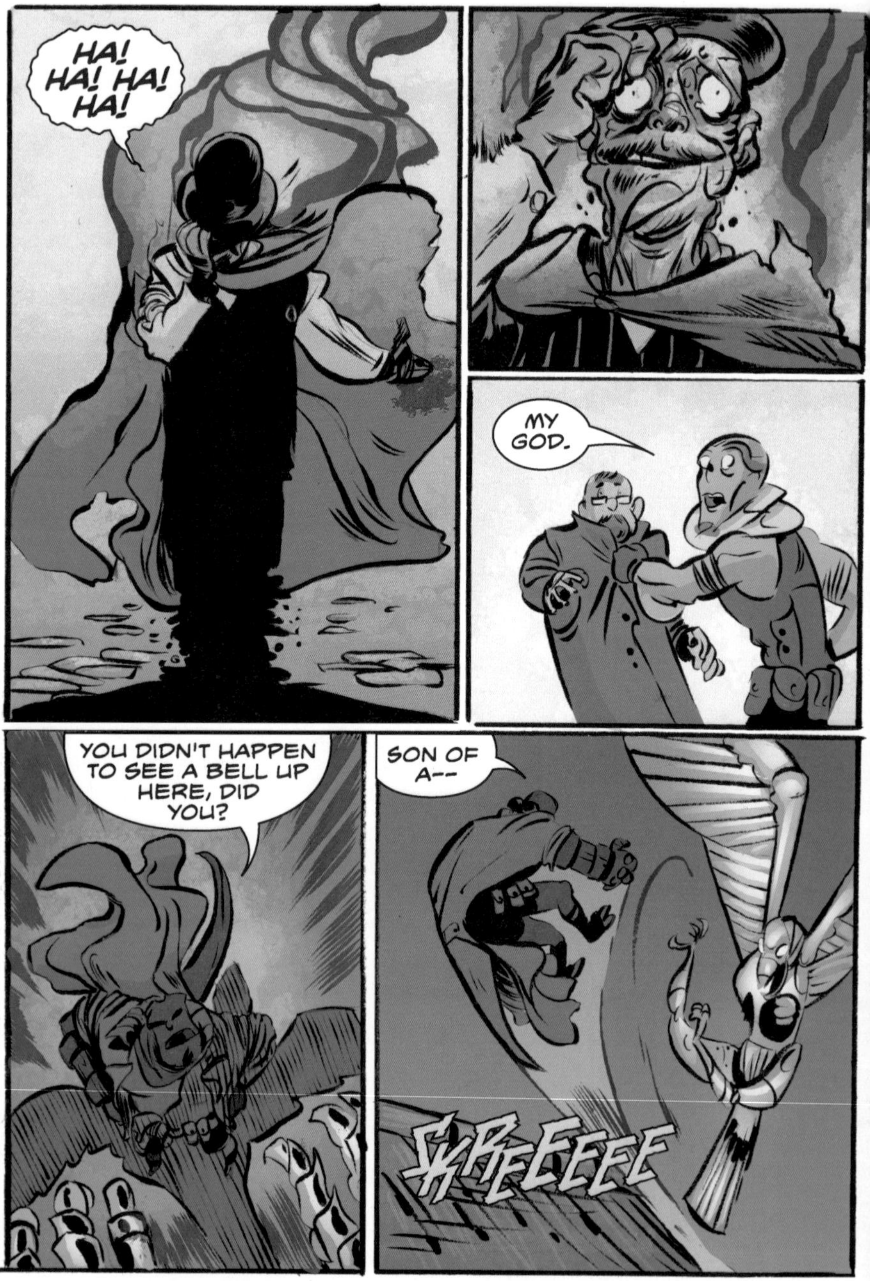
HA! HA! HA! HA!
MY GOD.
YOU DIDN'T HAPPEN TO SEE A BELL UP HERE, DID YOU?
SON OF A--
SKREEEEEE

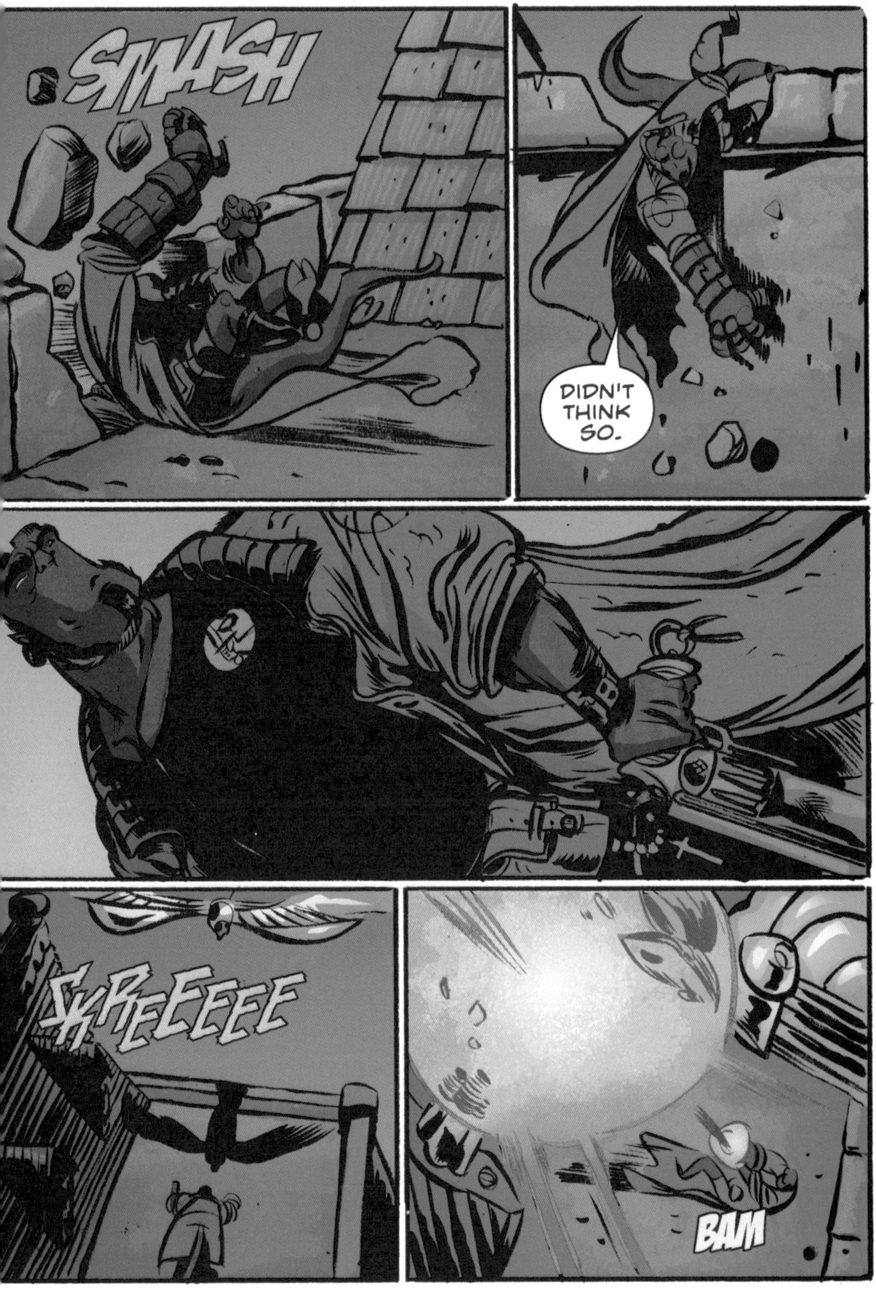
SMASH
DIDN'T THINK SO.
SKREEEEEE
BAM

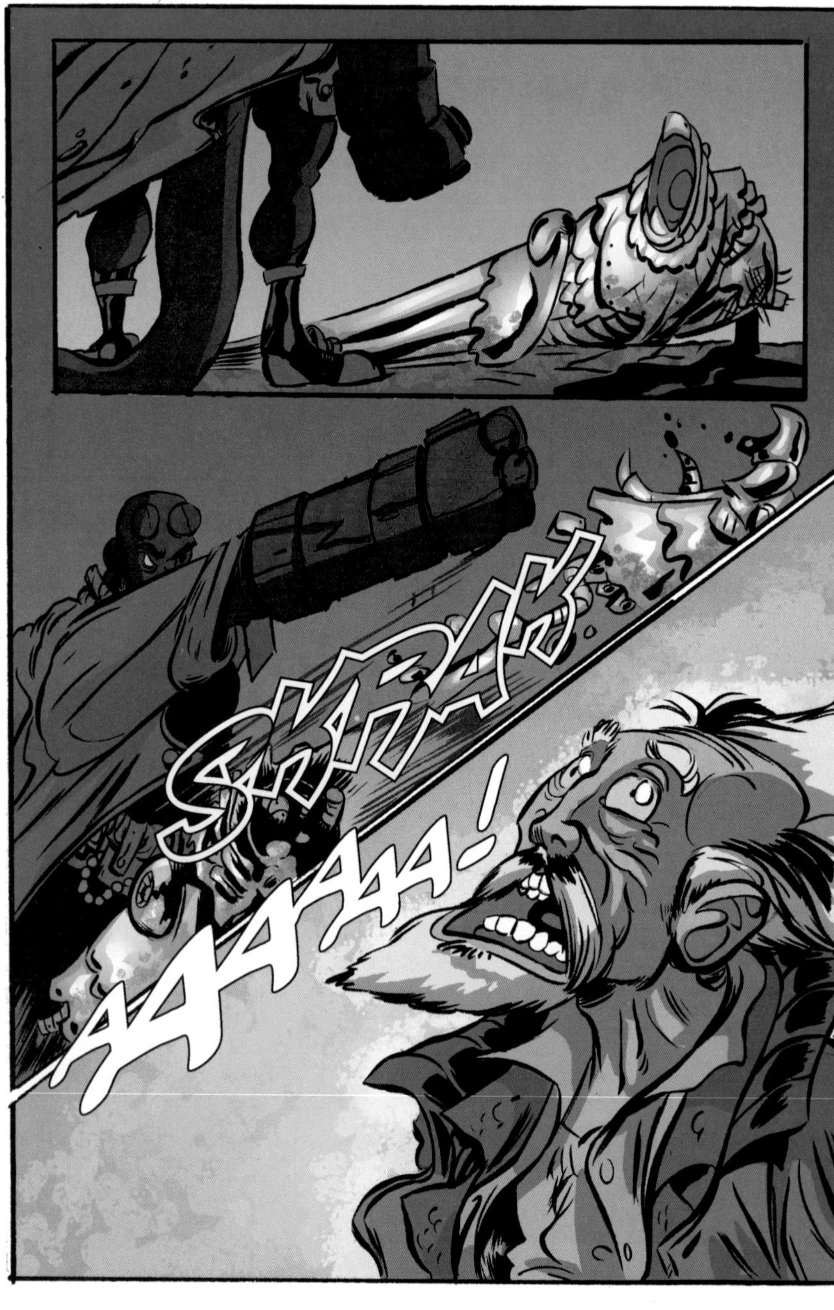
SHRAK
AAAAAA!

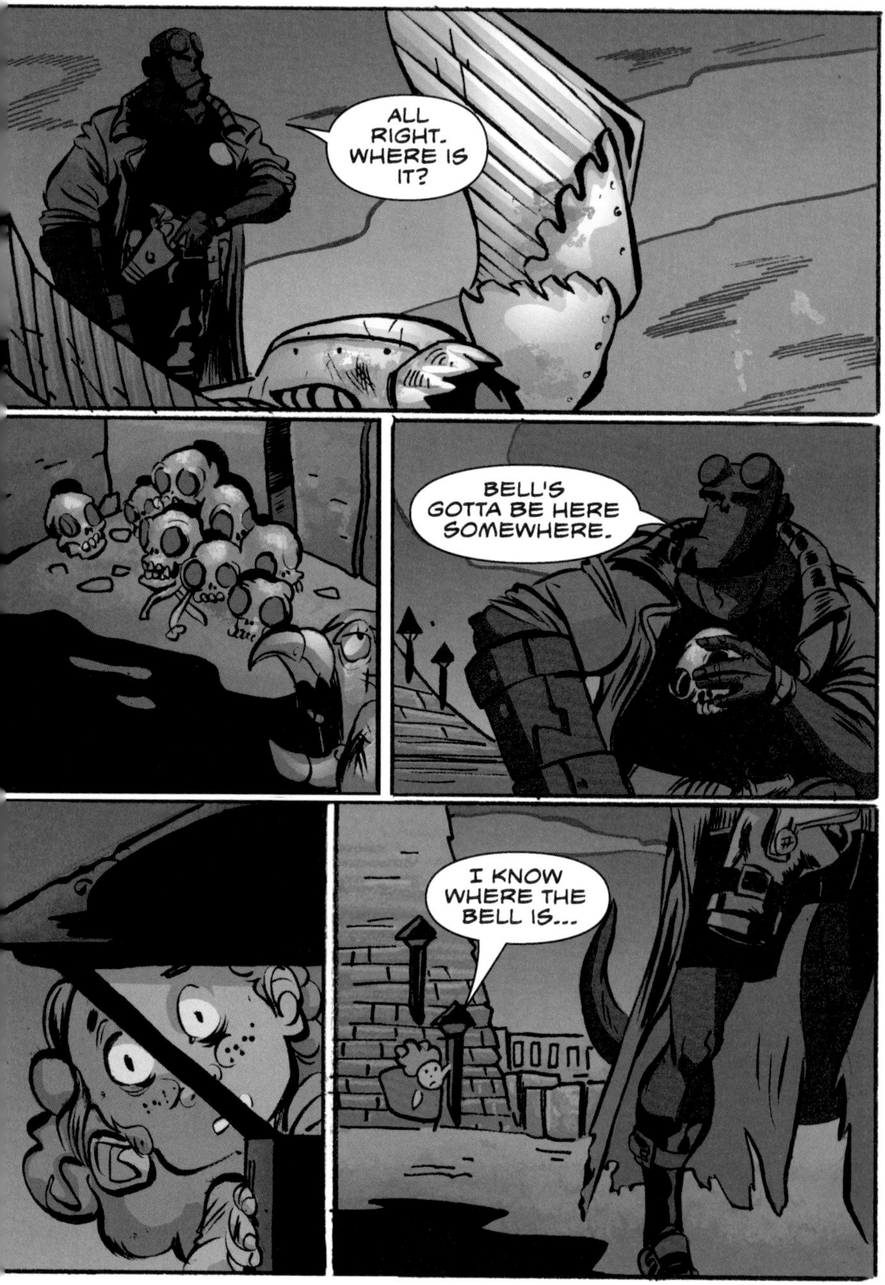
ALL RIGHT. WHERE IS IT?
BELL'S GOTTA BE HERE SOMEWHERE.
I KNOW WHERE THE BELL IS...

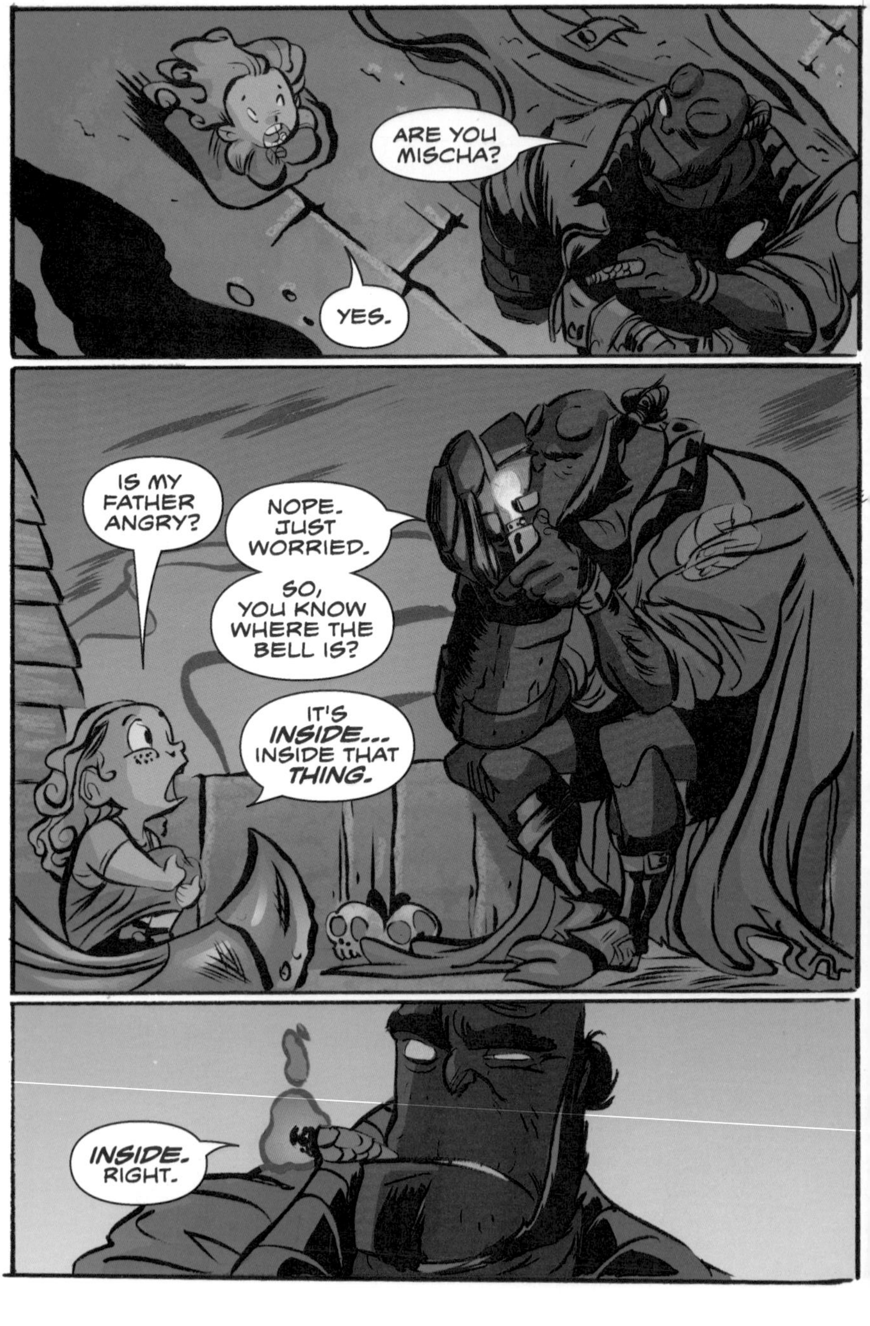
ARE YOU MISCHA?
YES.
IS MY FATHER ANGRY?
NOPE. JUST WORRIED.
SO, YOU KNOW WHERE THE BELL IS?
IT'S *INSIDE...* INSIDE THAT *THING.*
INSIDE. RIGHT.

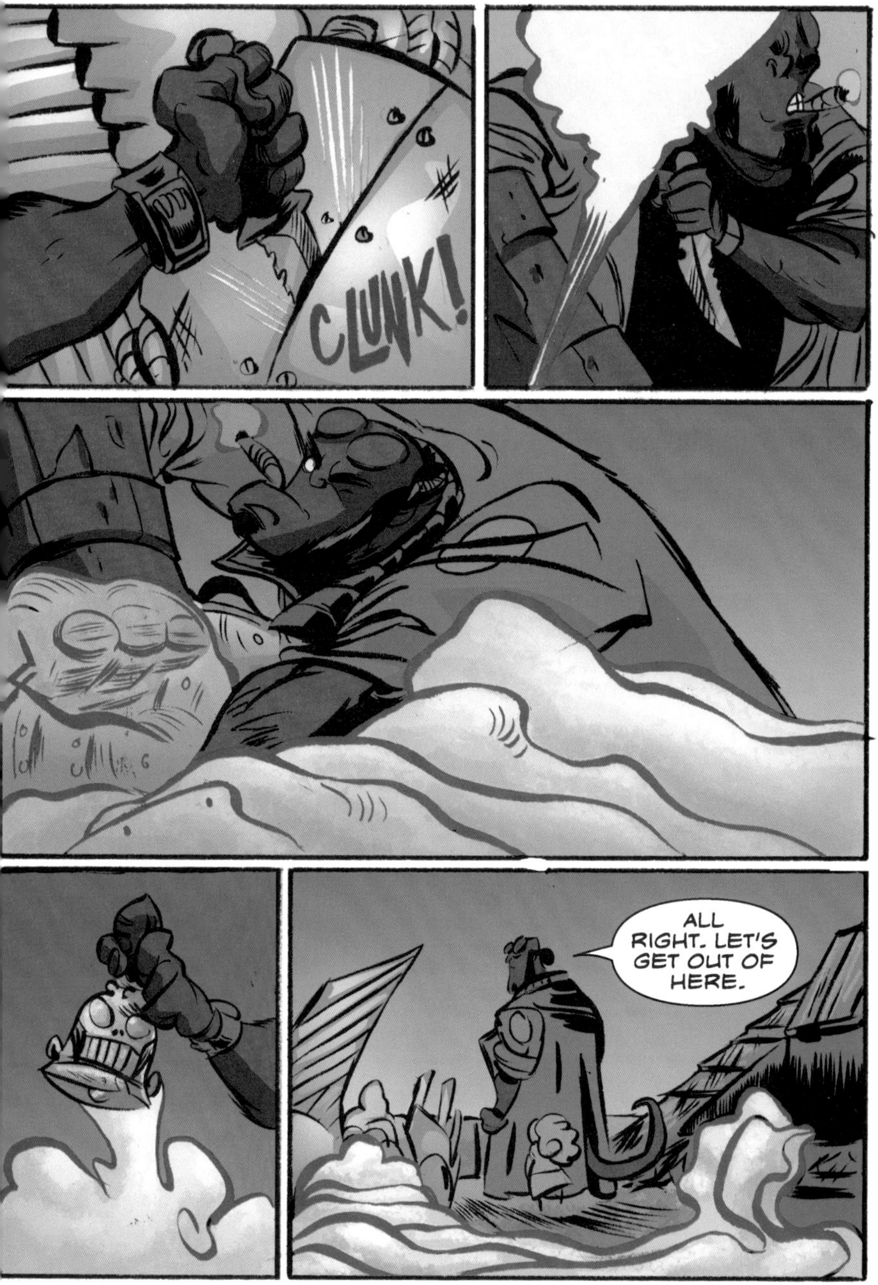
CLUNK!
ALL RIGHT. LET'S GET OUT OF HERE.

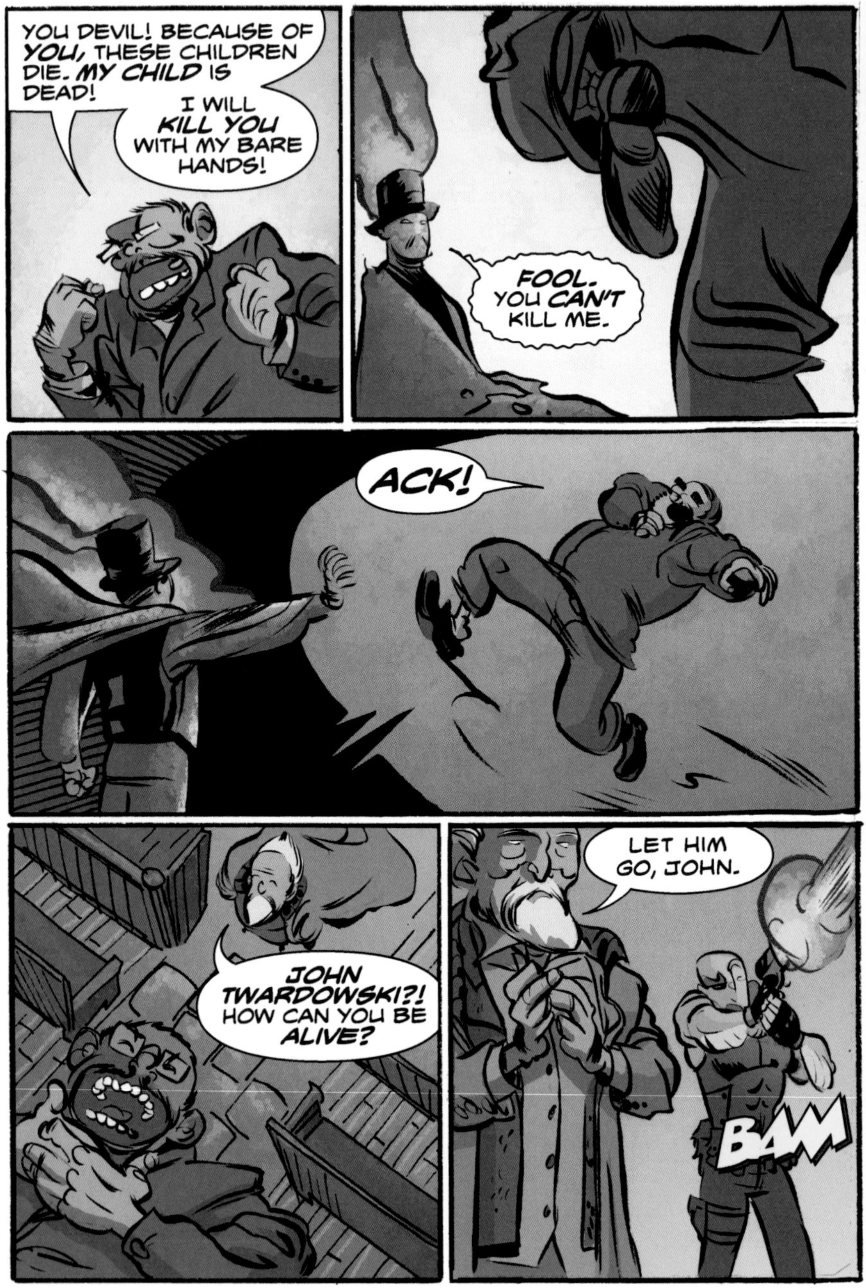
YOU DEVIL! BECAUSE OF YOU, THESE CHILDREN DIE. MY CHILD IS DEAD!
I WILL KILL YOU WITH MY BARE HANDS!
FOOL. YOU CAN'T KILL ME.
ACK!
JOHN TWARDOWSKI?! HOW CAN YOU BE ALIVE?
LET HIM GO, JOHN.
BAM

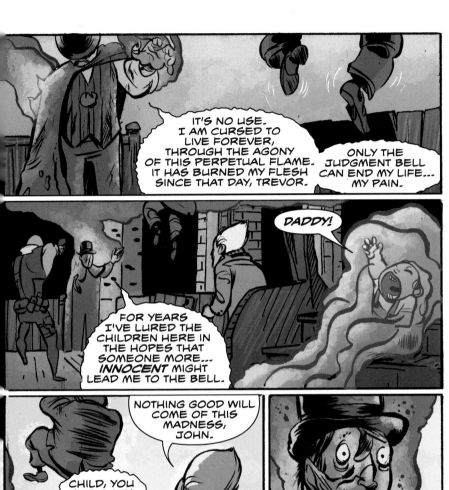

IT'S NO USE. I AM CURSED TO LIVE FOREVER, THROUGH THE AGONY OF THIS PERPETUAL FLAME. IT HAS BURNED MY FLESH SINCE THAT DAY, TREVOR.

ONLY THE JUDGMENT BELL CAN END MY LIFE... MY PAIN.

DADDY!

FOR YEARS I'VE LURED THE CHILDREN HERE IN THE HOPES THAT SOMEONE MORE... *INNOCENT* MIGHT LEAD ME TO THE BELL.

NOTHING GOOD WILL COME OF THIS MADNESS, JOHN.

CHILD, YOU SURVIVED! WHERE IS THE BELL?

IT'S ALL YOUR FAULT, TREVOR! YOU COULD NEVER HOPE TO--

YOU!

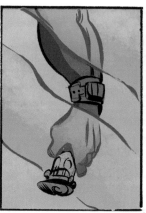

I SAW YOU DESTROYED ALL THOSE YEARS AGO!

HOW... HOW DID YOU GET THE BELL BACK?

ANSWER ME, DEMON!

OOF!

I'M NOT YOUR DEMON.

GOOD TO SEE YOU ON YOUR FEET, SIR.

YOU KNOW THIS JOKER?

WHEN I WAS A YOUNG MAN, I MADE THE MISTAKE OF HELPING HIM TRICK A DEMON.

FOR MY PART IN WHAT YOU'VE BECOME, I'M SORRY, JOHN. BUT THIS ENDS NOW!

SO, YOU'VE MADE YOUR OWN DEAL WITH THIS MONSTER! I WOULD NEVER HAVE THOUGHT YOU COULD DO IT.

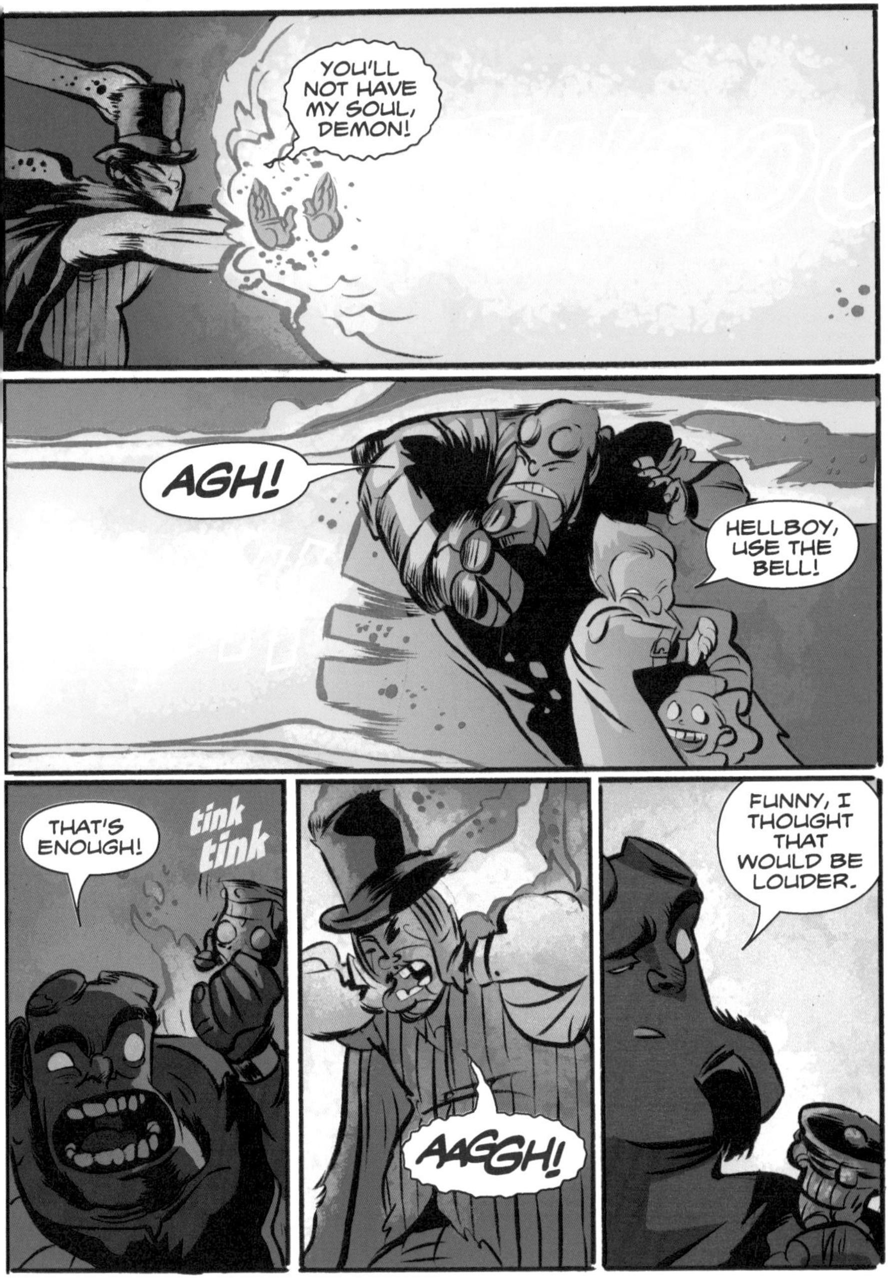
YOU'LL NOT HAVE MY SOUL, DEMON!
AGH!
HELLBOY, USE THE BELL!
THAT'S ENOUGH!
tink tink
AAGGH!
FUNNY, I THOUGHT THAT WOULD BE LOUDER.

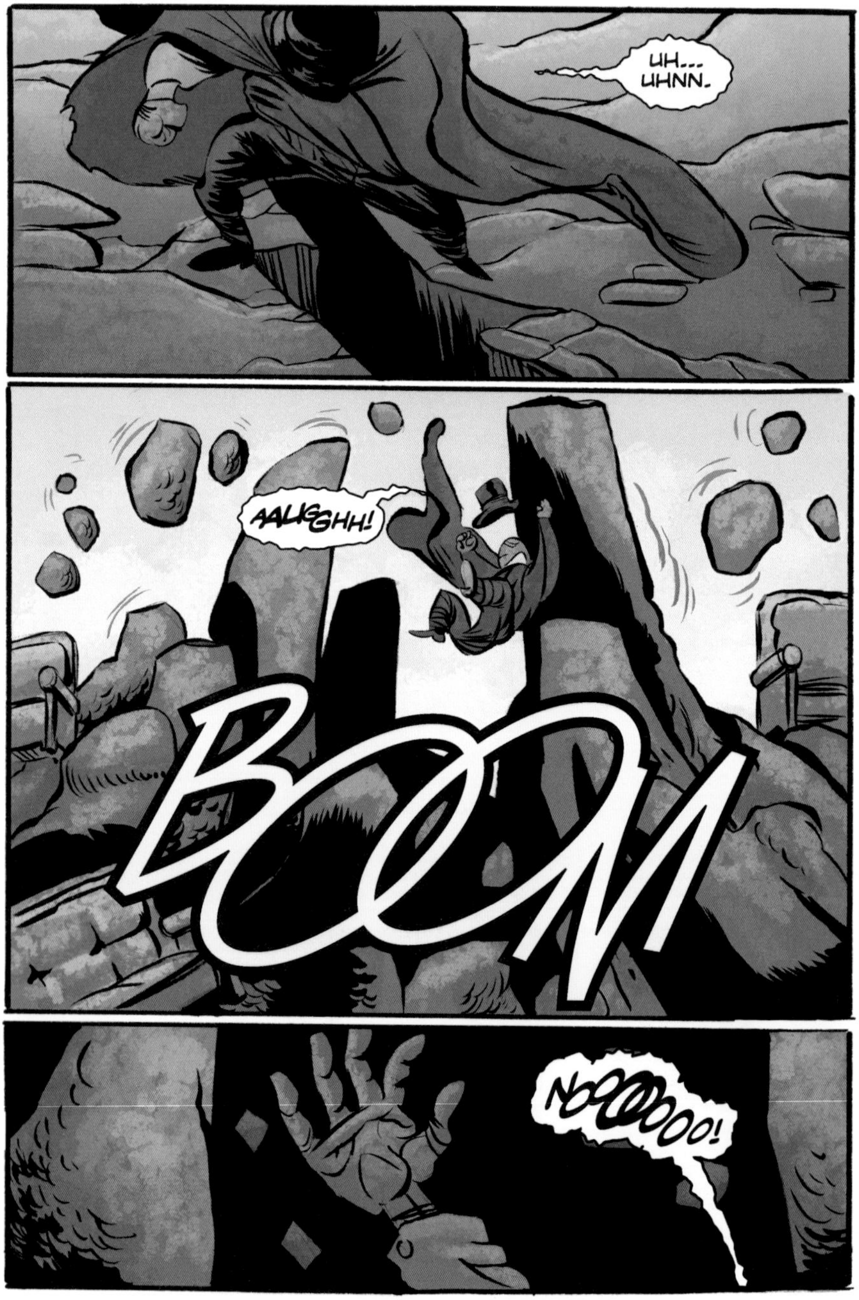
UH... UHNN.
AAUGGHH!
BOOM
NOOOOOOO!

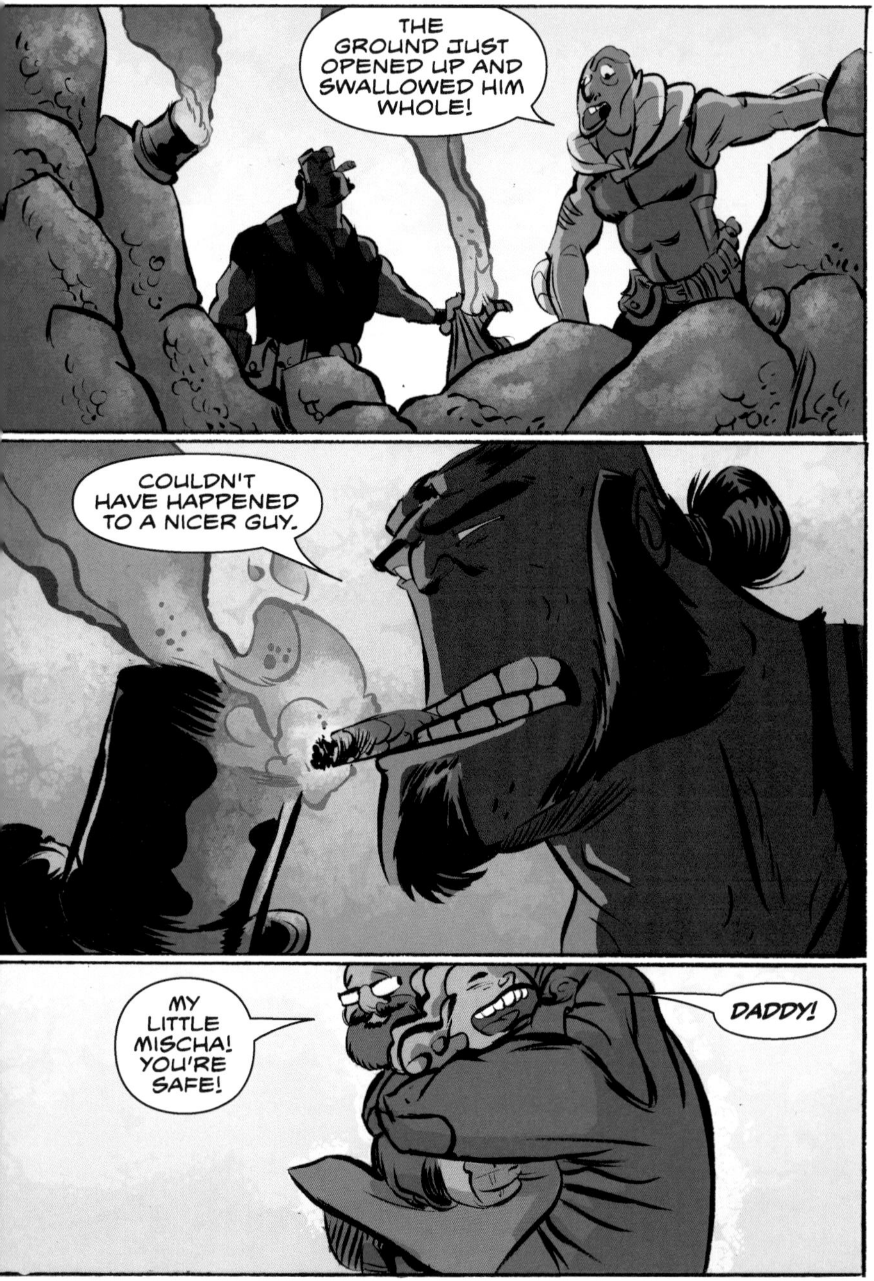
THE GROUND JUST OPENED UP AND SWALLOWED HIM WHOLE!
COULDN'T HAVE HAPPENED TO A NICER GUY.
MY LITTLE MISCHA! YOU'RE SAFE!
DADDY!

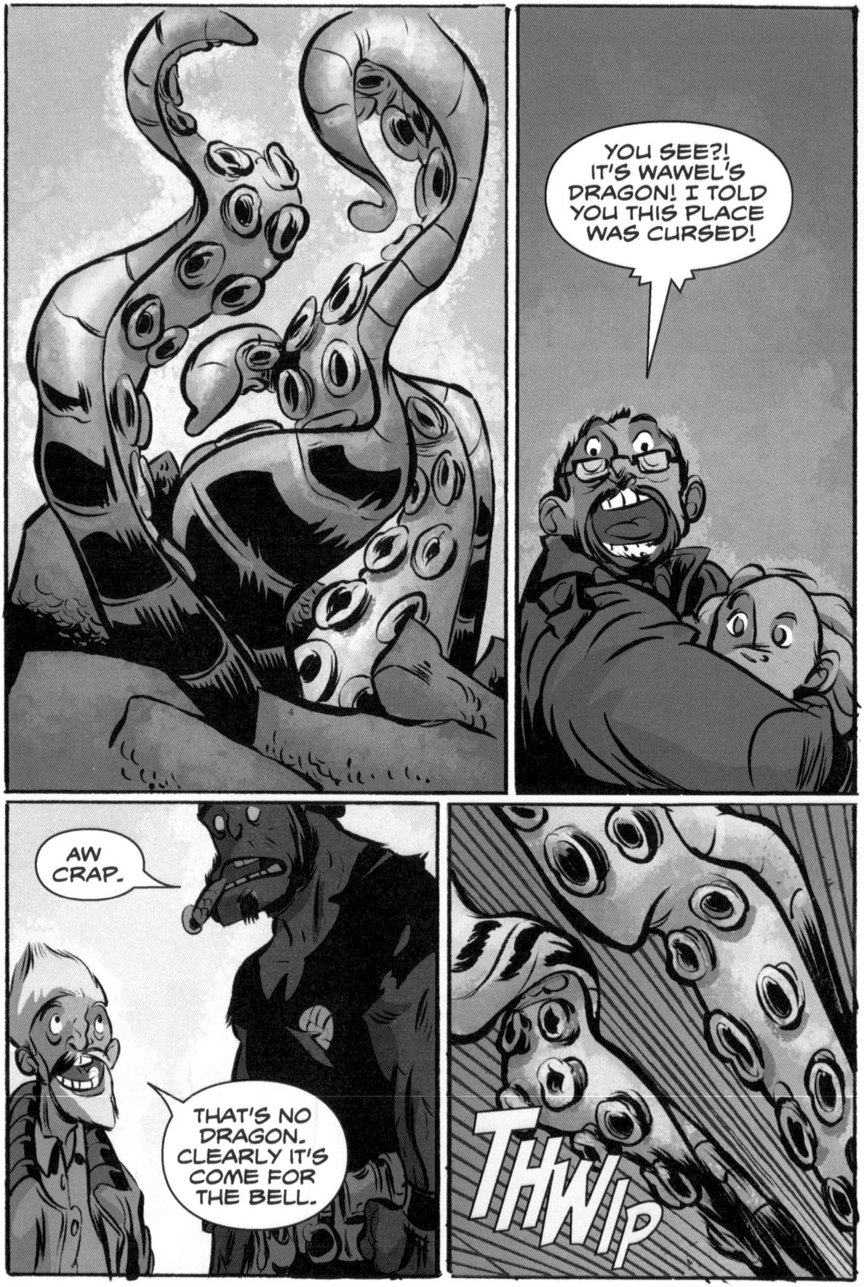
YOU SEE?! IT'S WAWEL'S DRAGON! I TOLD YOU THIS PLACE WAS CURSED!
AW CRAP.
THAT'S NO DRAGON. CLEARLY IT'S COME FOR THE BELL.
THWIP

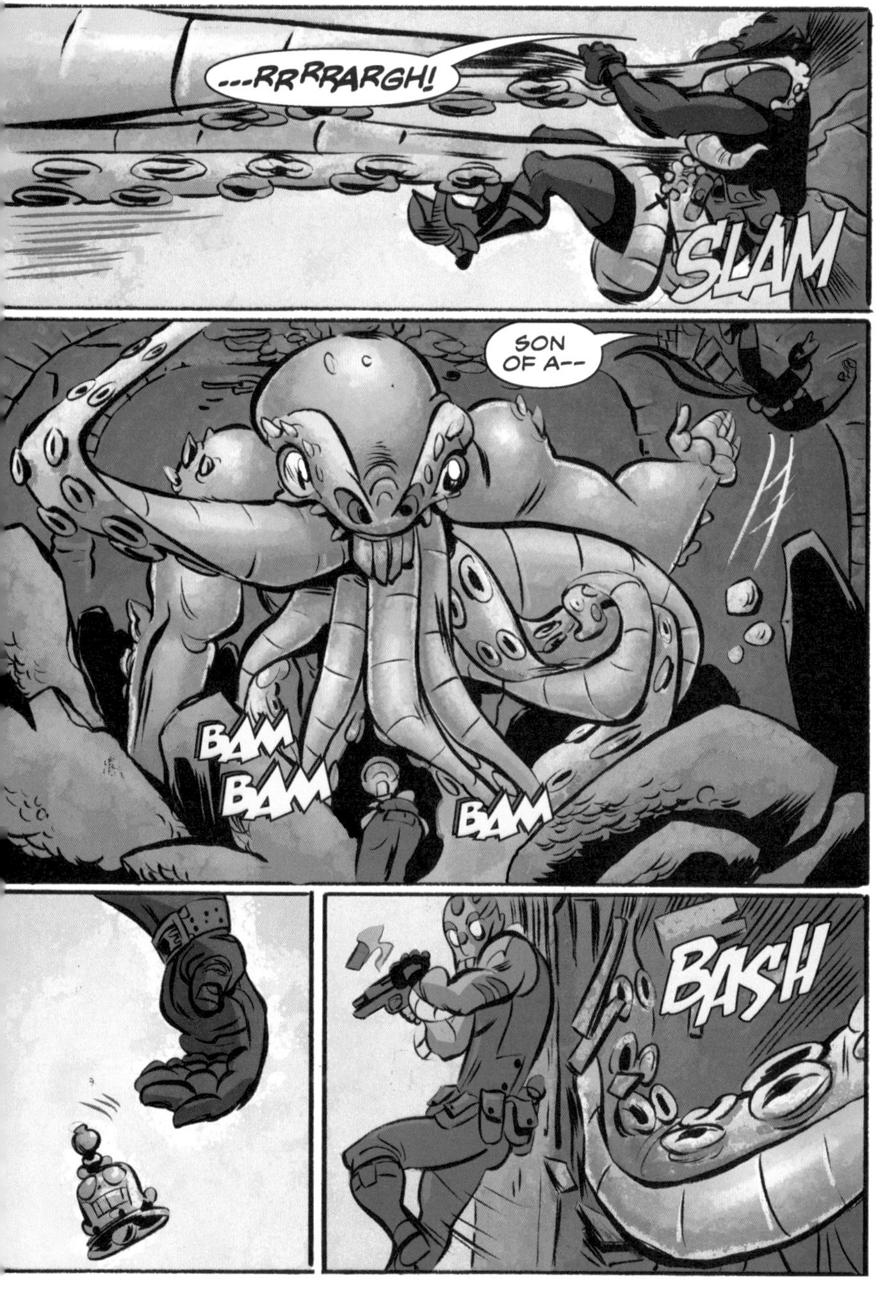

---RRRRRARGH!
SLAM
SON OF A--
BAM
BAM
BAM
BASH

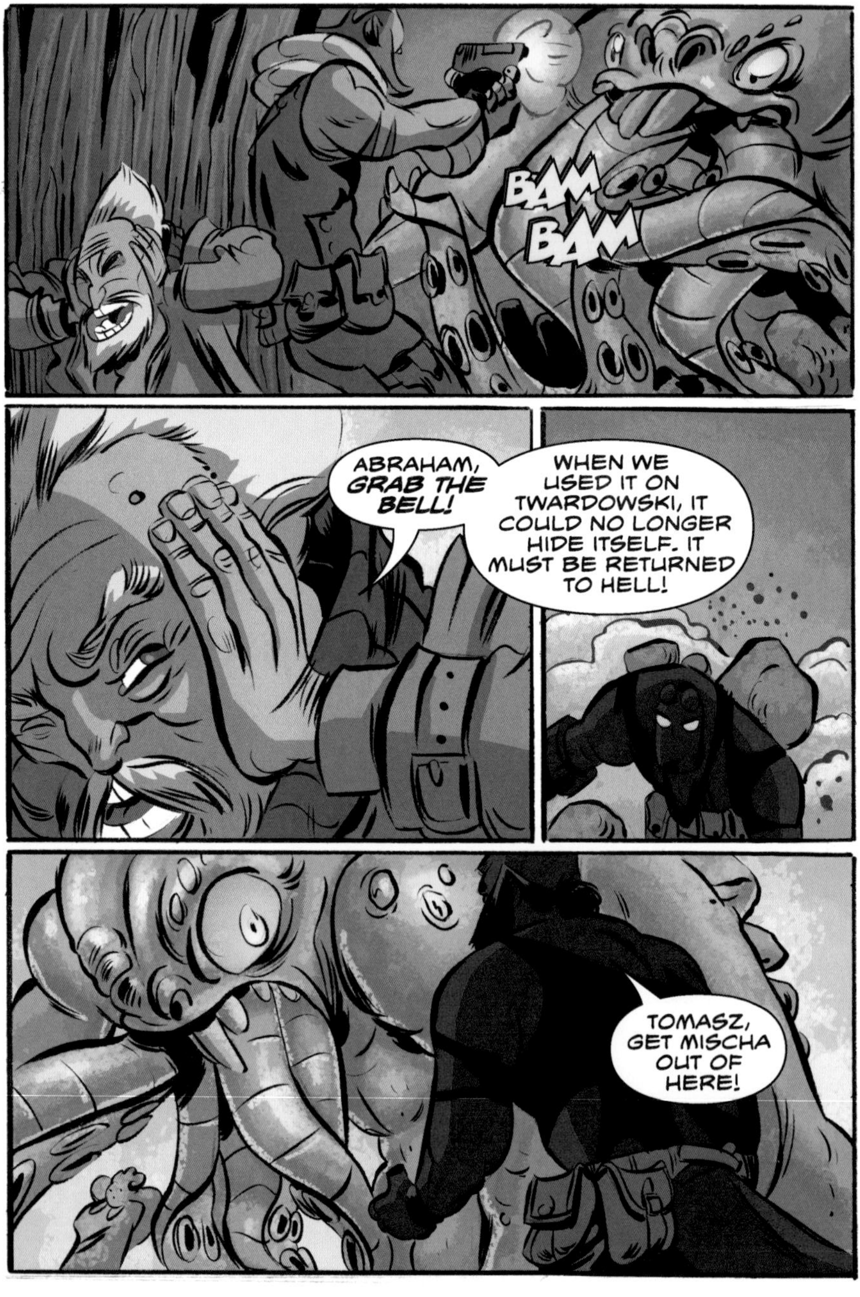
BAM
BAM
ABRAHAM, GRAB THE BELL!
WHEN WE USED IT ON TWARDOWSKI, IT COULD NO LONGER HIDE ITSELF. IT MUST BE RETURNED TO HELL!
TOMASZ, GET MISCHA OUT OF HERE!

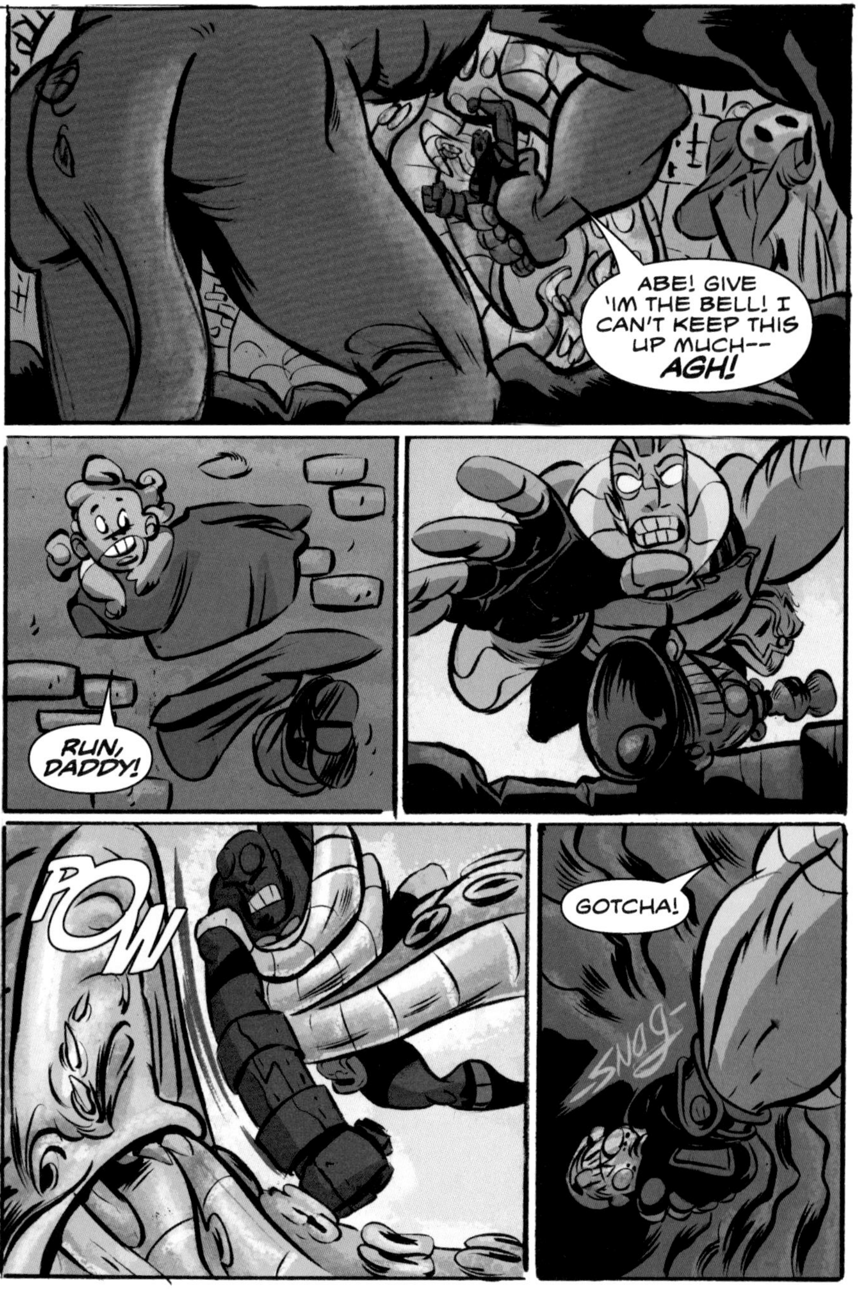
ABE! GIVE 'IM THE BELL! I CAN'T KEEP THIS UP MUCH-- AGH!
RUN, DADDY!
POW
GOTCHA!
SNAG-

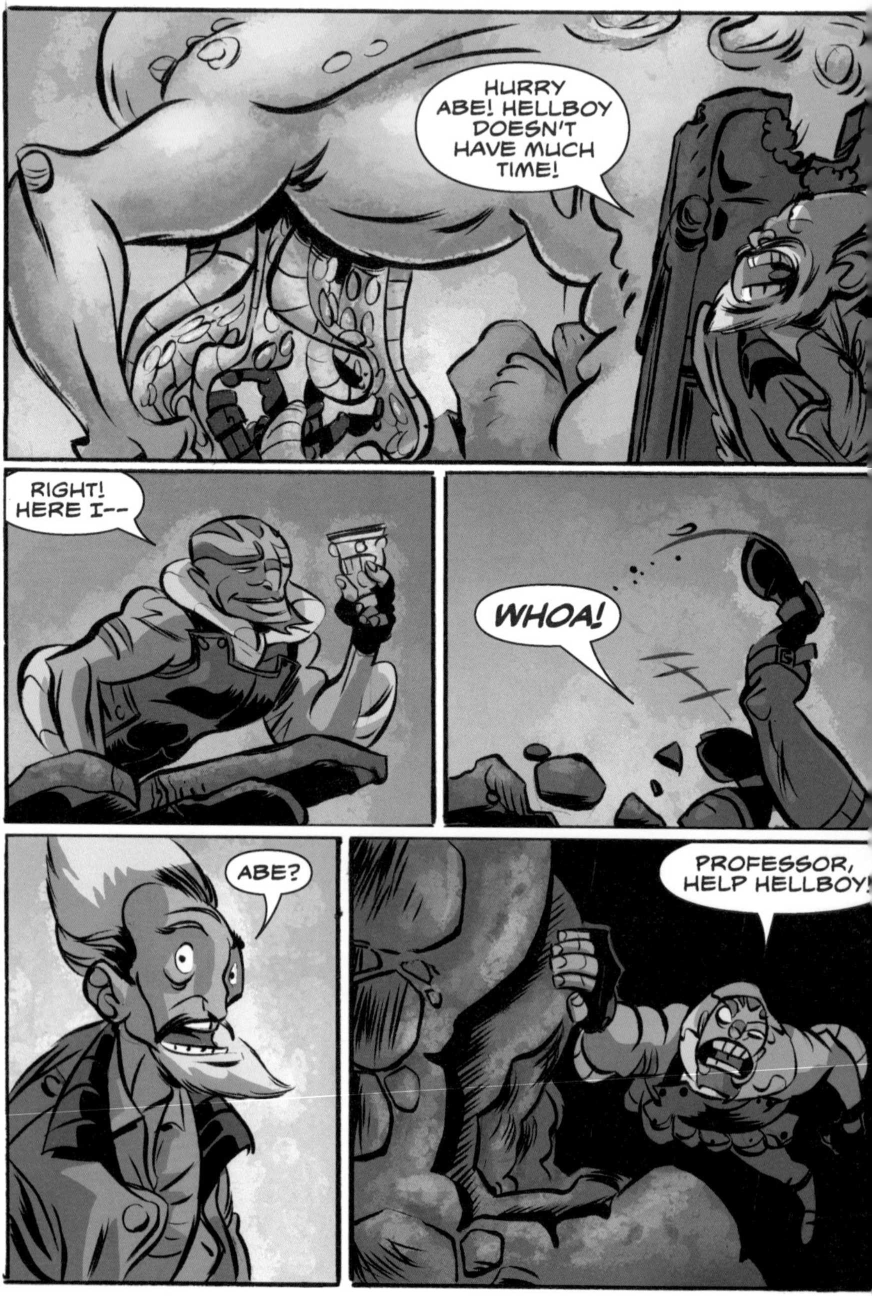
HURRY ABE! HELLBOY DOESN'T HAVE MUCH TIME!
RIGHT! HERE I--
WHOA!
ABE?
PROFESSOR, HELP HELLBOY!

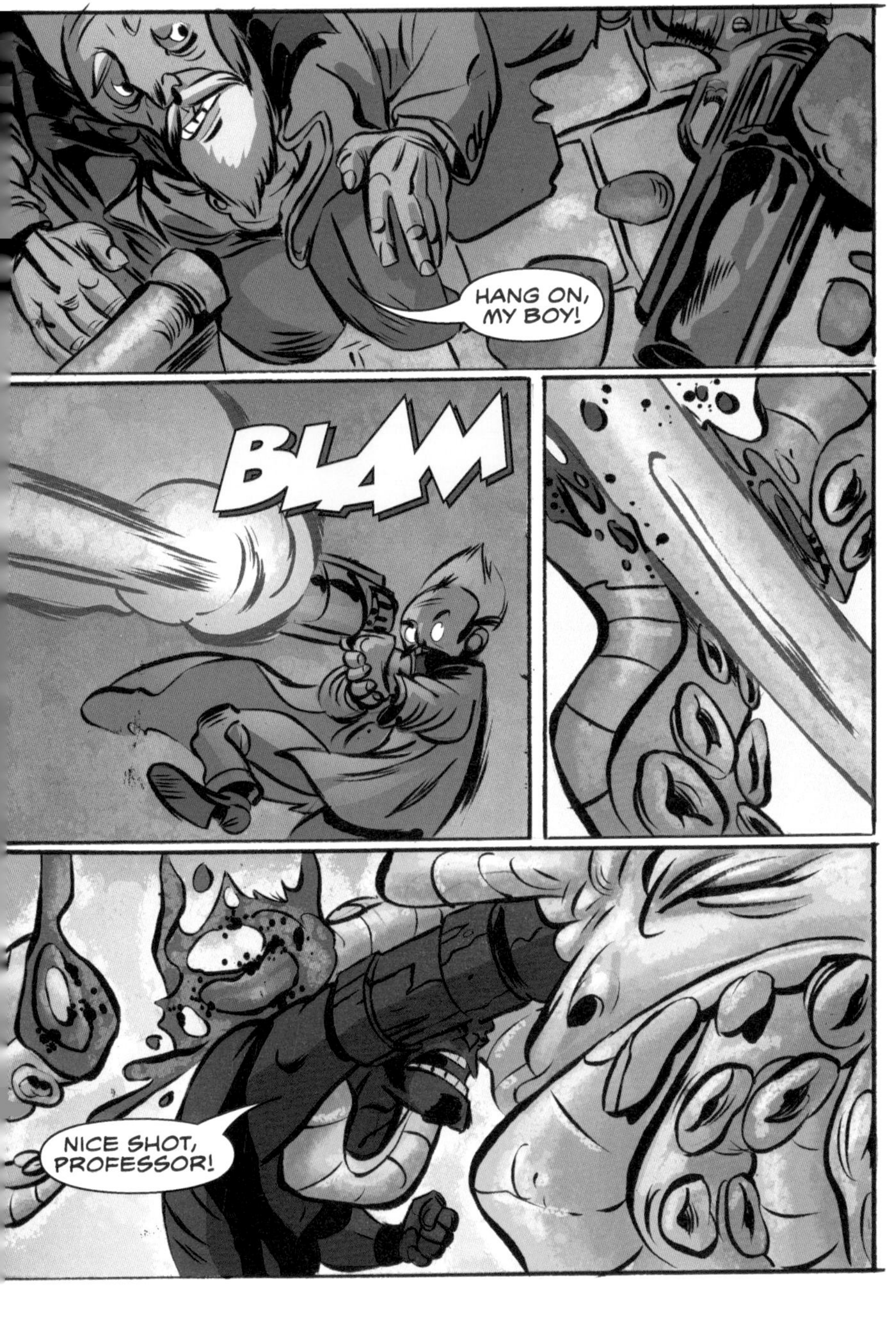
HANG ON, MY BOY!
BLAM
NICE SHOT, PROFESSOR!

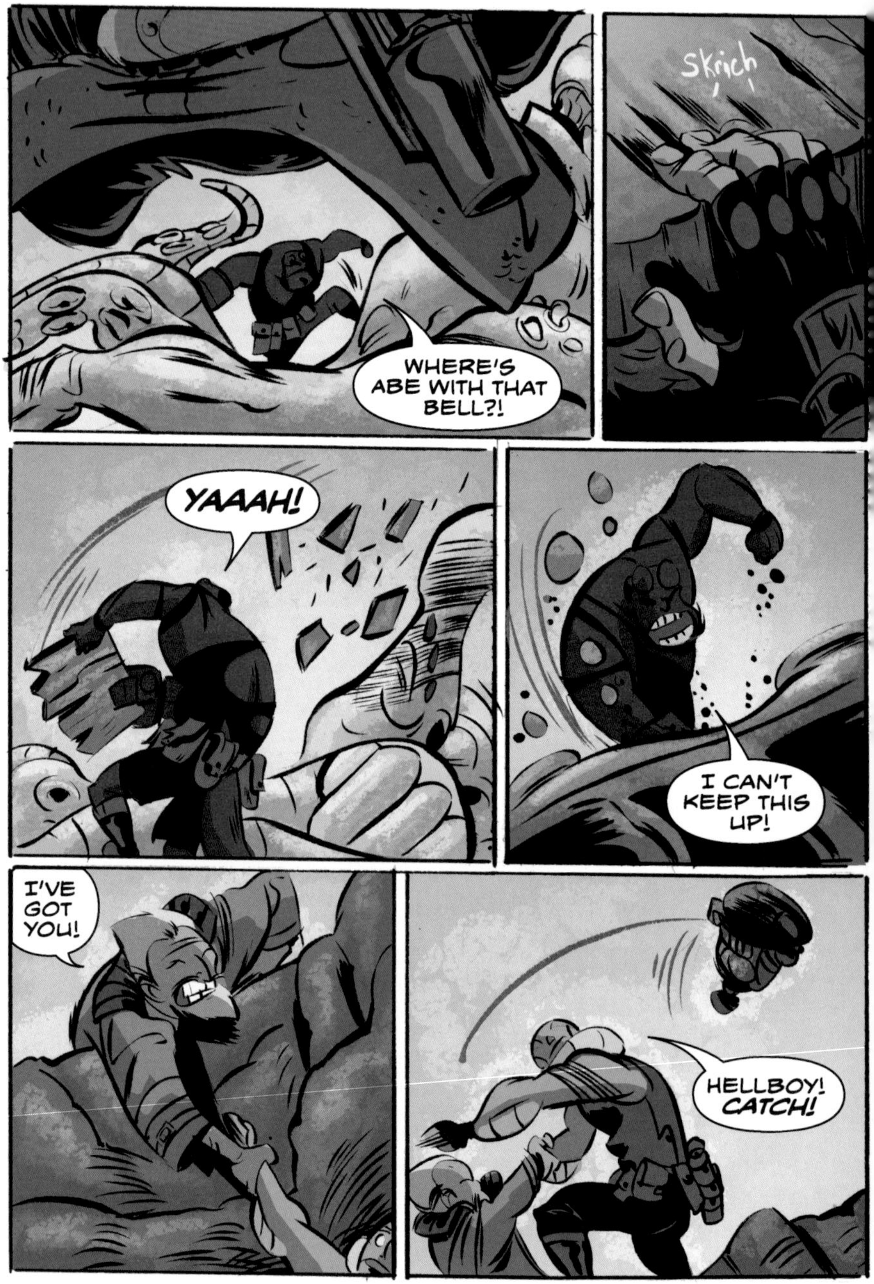
WHERE'S ABE WITH THAT BELL?!
SKRICH
YAAAH!
I CAN'T KEEP THIS UP!
I'VE GOT YOU!
HELLBOY! CATCH!

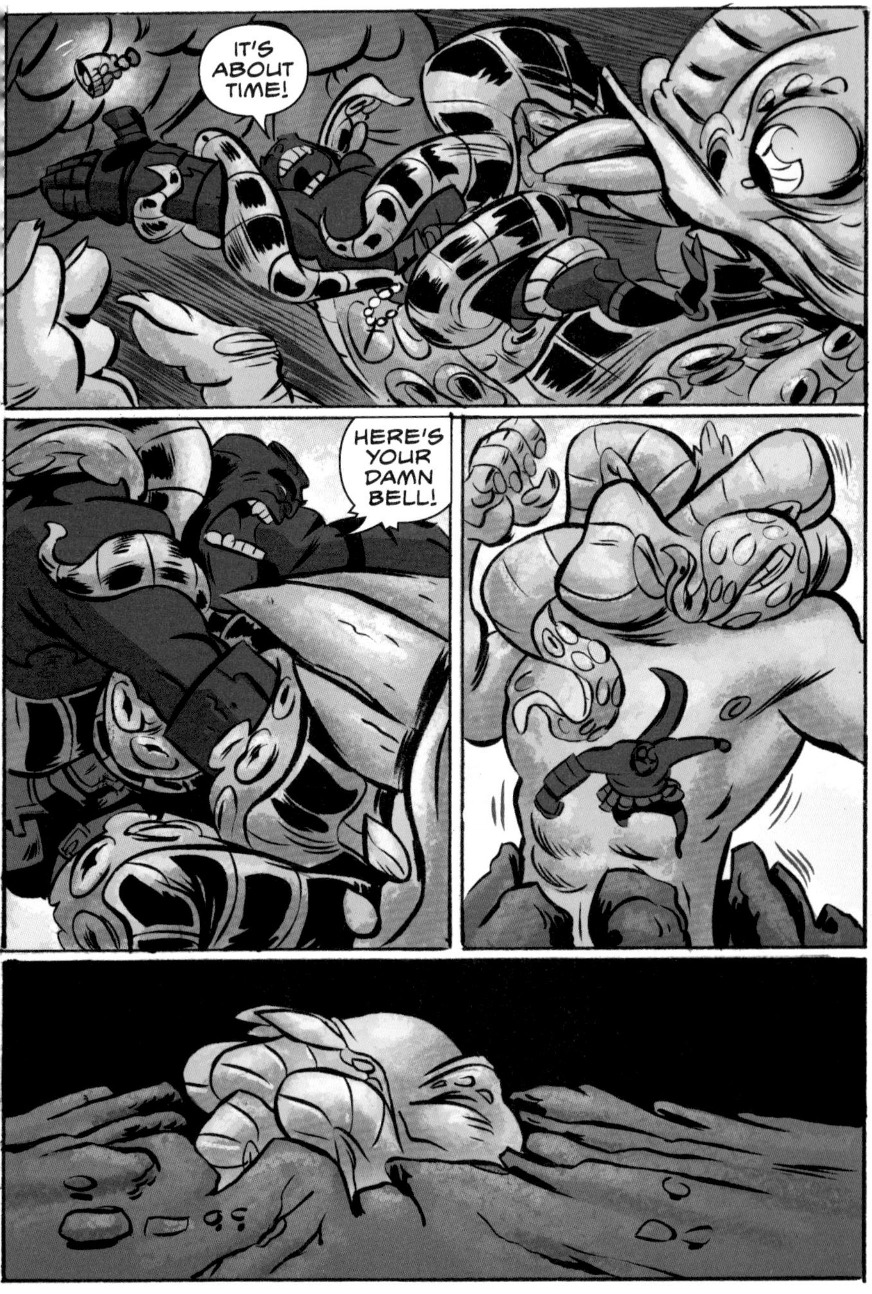
IT'S ABOUT TIME!
HERE'S YOUR DAMN BELL!

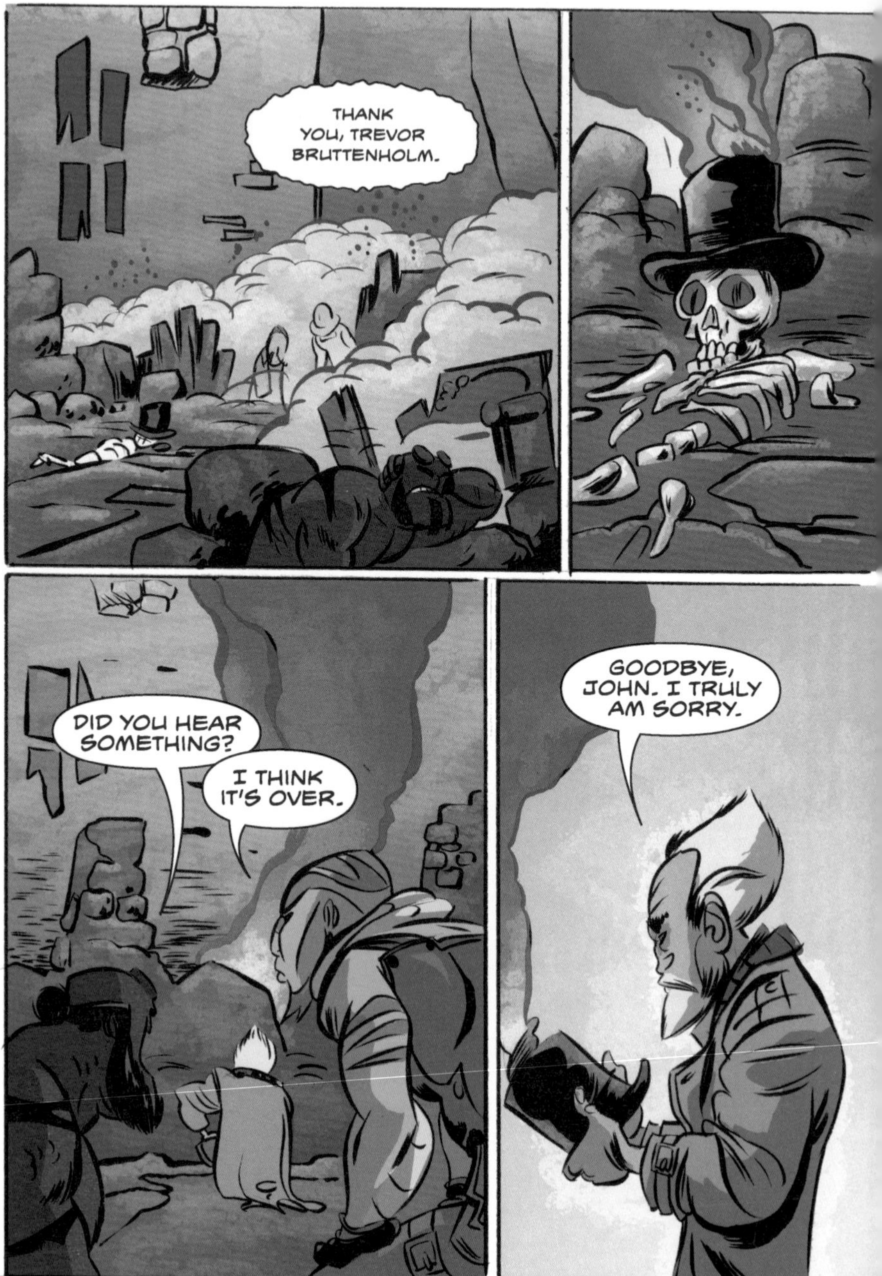
THANK YOU, TREVOR BRUTTENHOLM.
DID YOU HEAR SOMETHING?
I THINK IT'S OVER.
GOODBYE, JOHN. I TRULY AM SORRY.

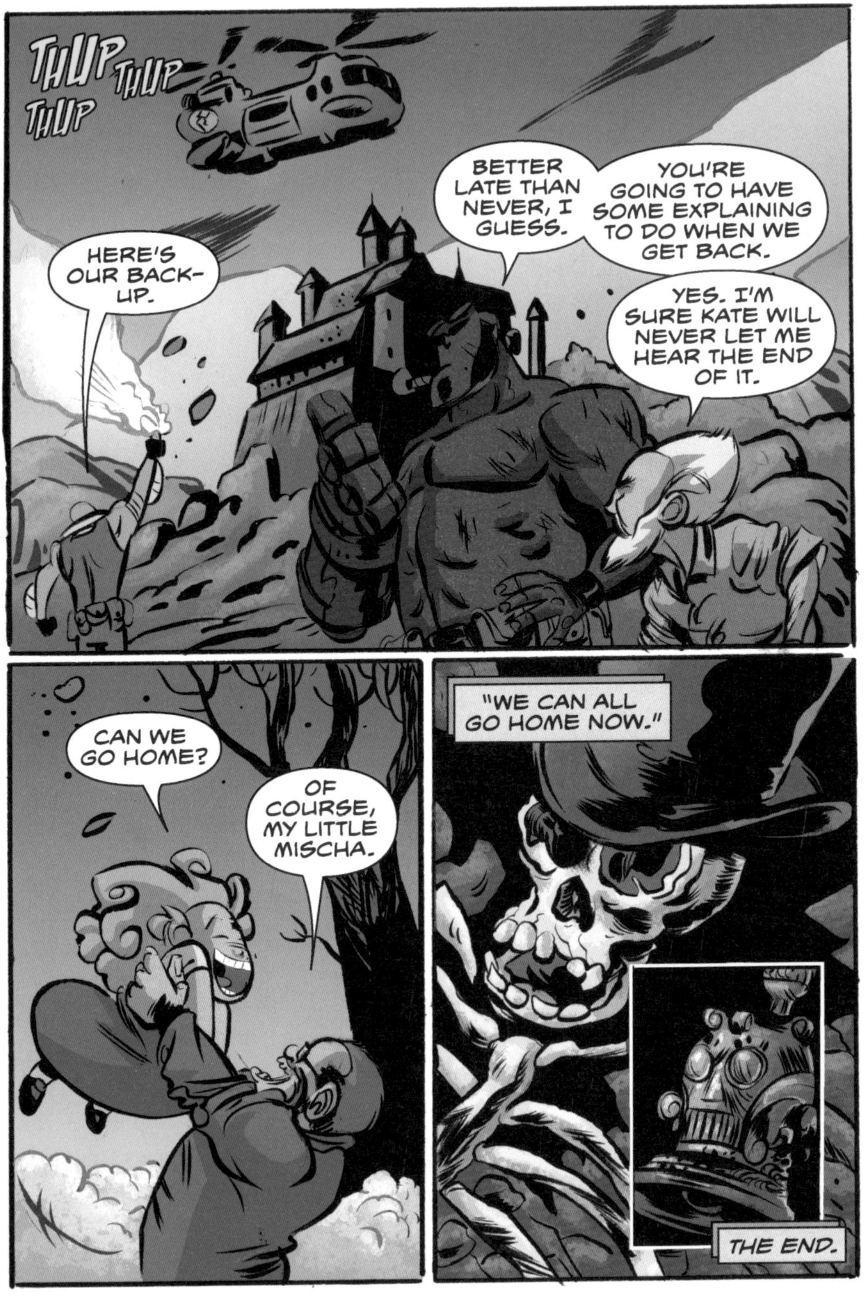
THUP THUP THUP
HERE'S OUR BACK-UP.
BETTER LATE THAN NEVER, I GUESS.
YOU'RE GOING TO HAVE SOME EXPLAINING TO DO WHEN WE GET BACK.
YES. I'M SURE KATE WILL NEVER LET ME HEAR THE END OF IT.
CAN WE GO HOME?
OF COURSE, MY LITTLE MISCHA.
"WE CAN ALL GO HOME NOW."
THE END.

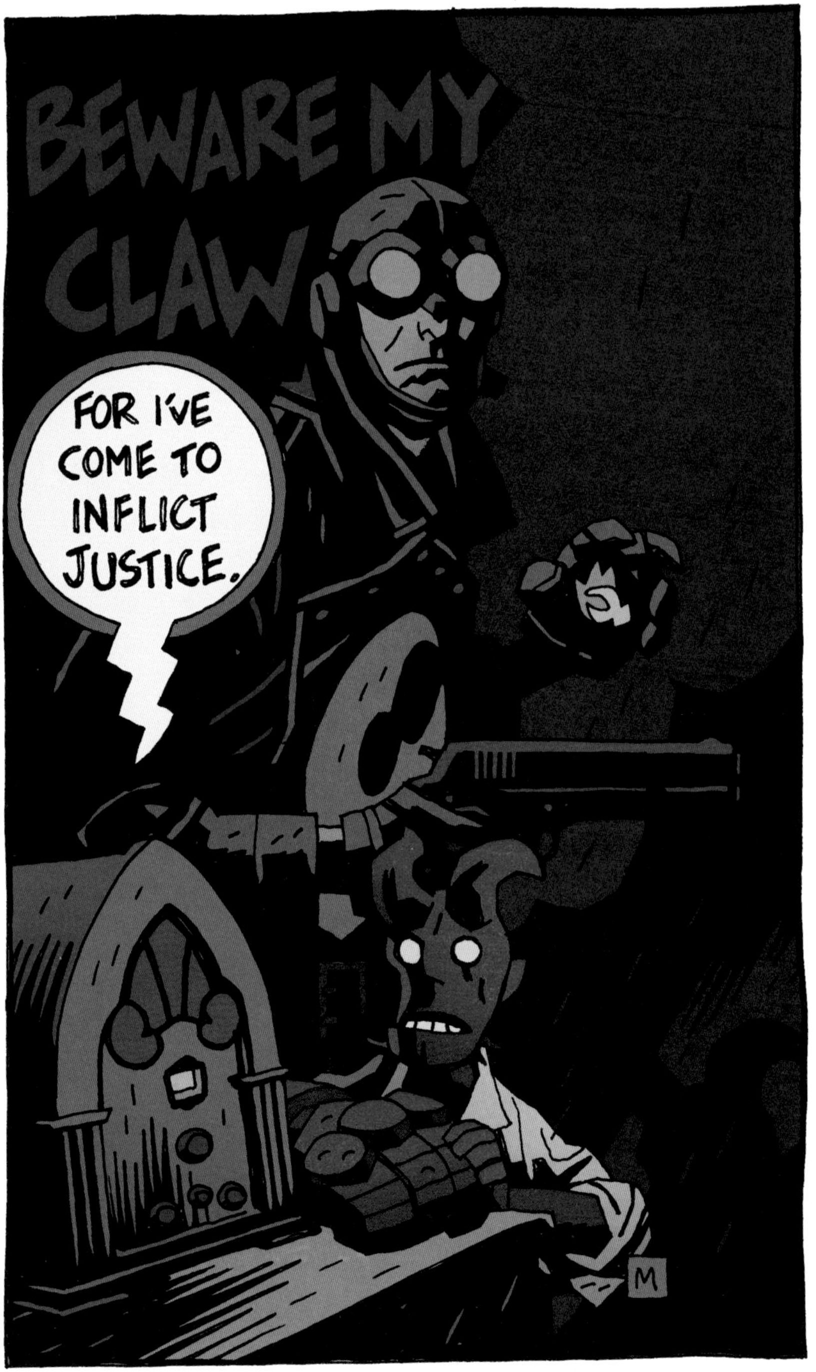
BEWARE MY CLAW
FOR I'VE COME TO INFLICT JUSTICE.
M

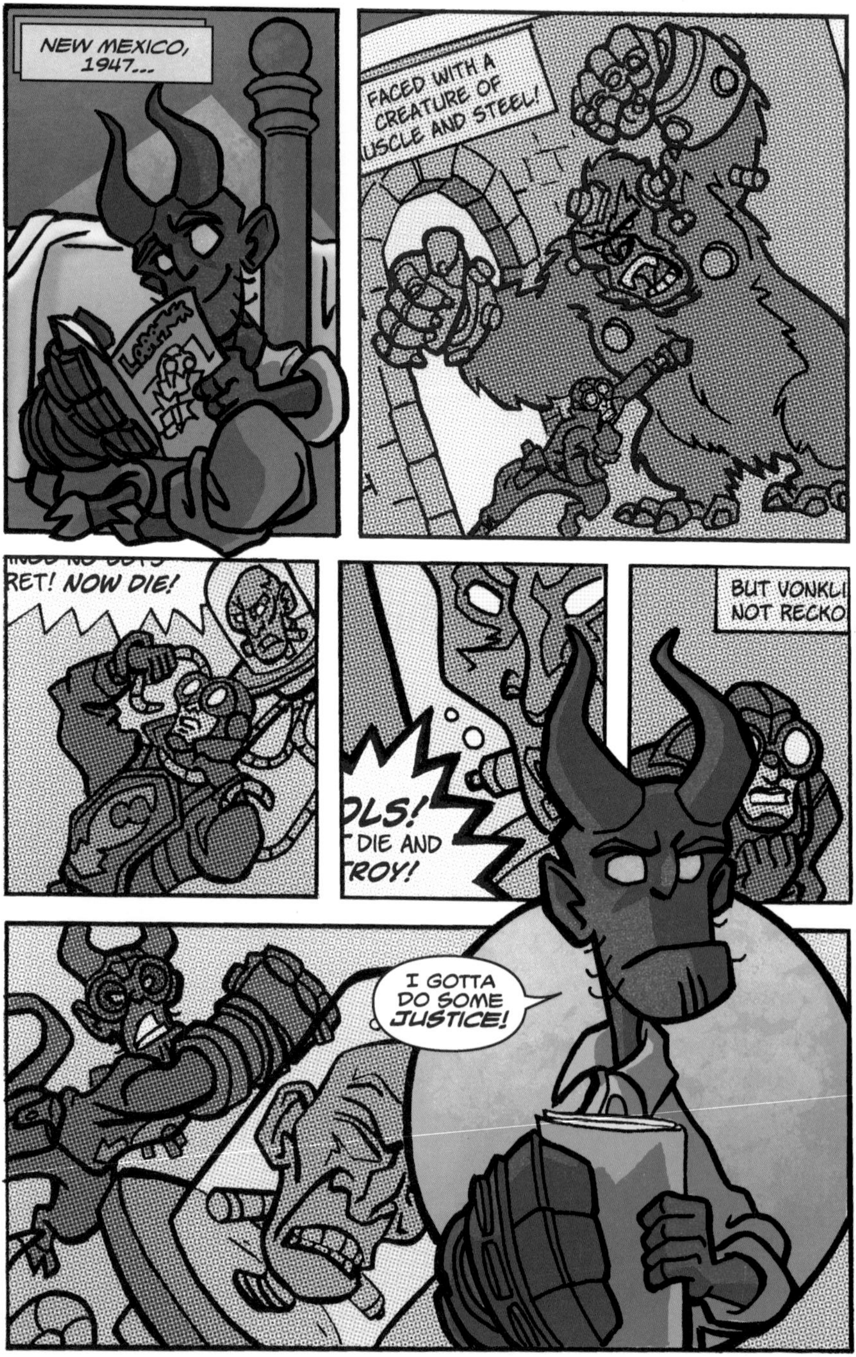
NEW MEXICO, 1947...
FACED WITH A CREATURE OF USCLE AND STEEL!
RET! NOW DIE!
OLS! T DIE AND TROY!
BUT VONKLI NOT RECKO
I GOTTA DO SOME JUSTICE!

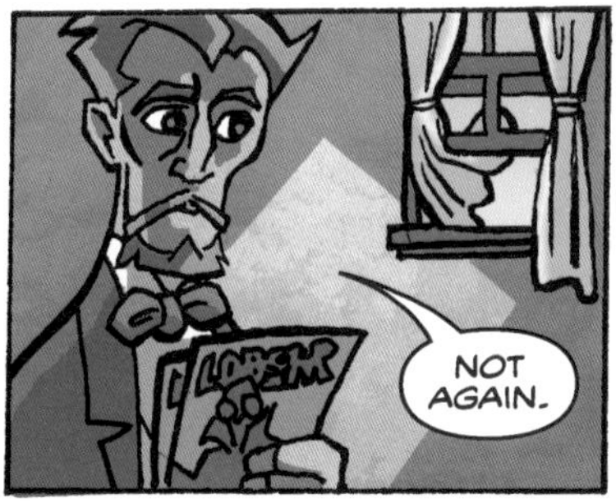
NOT AGAIN.

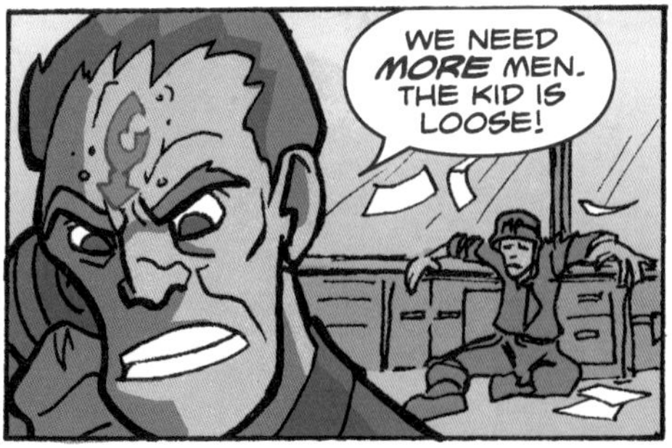
WE NEED MORE MEN. THE KID IS LOOSE!

THE MENACE OF THE MECHANICAL MONSTER

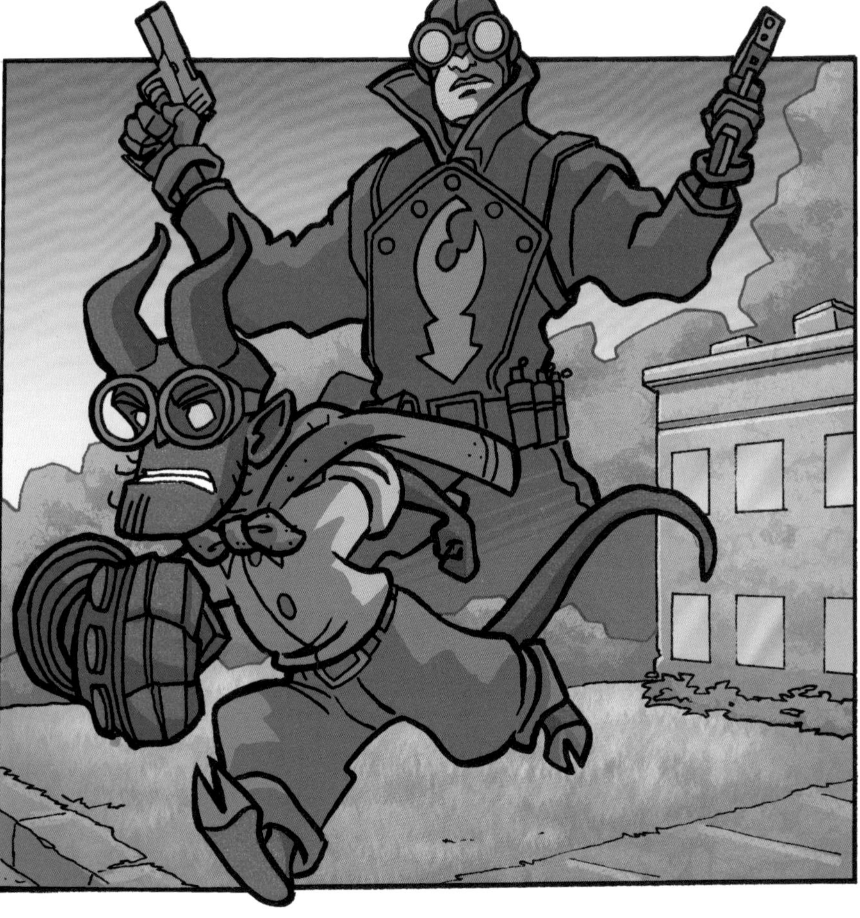

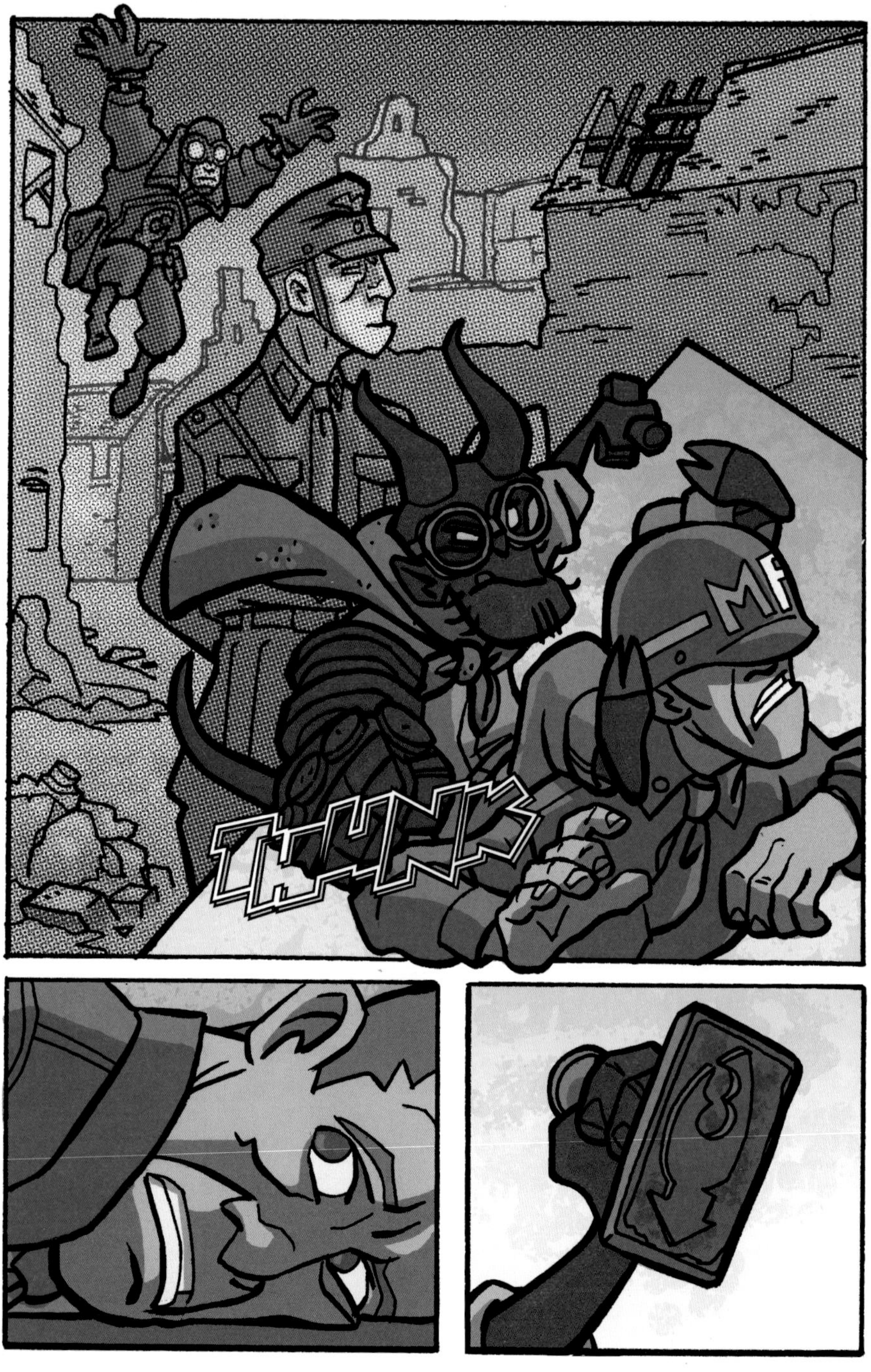
THUNK
MP

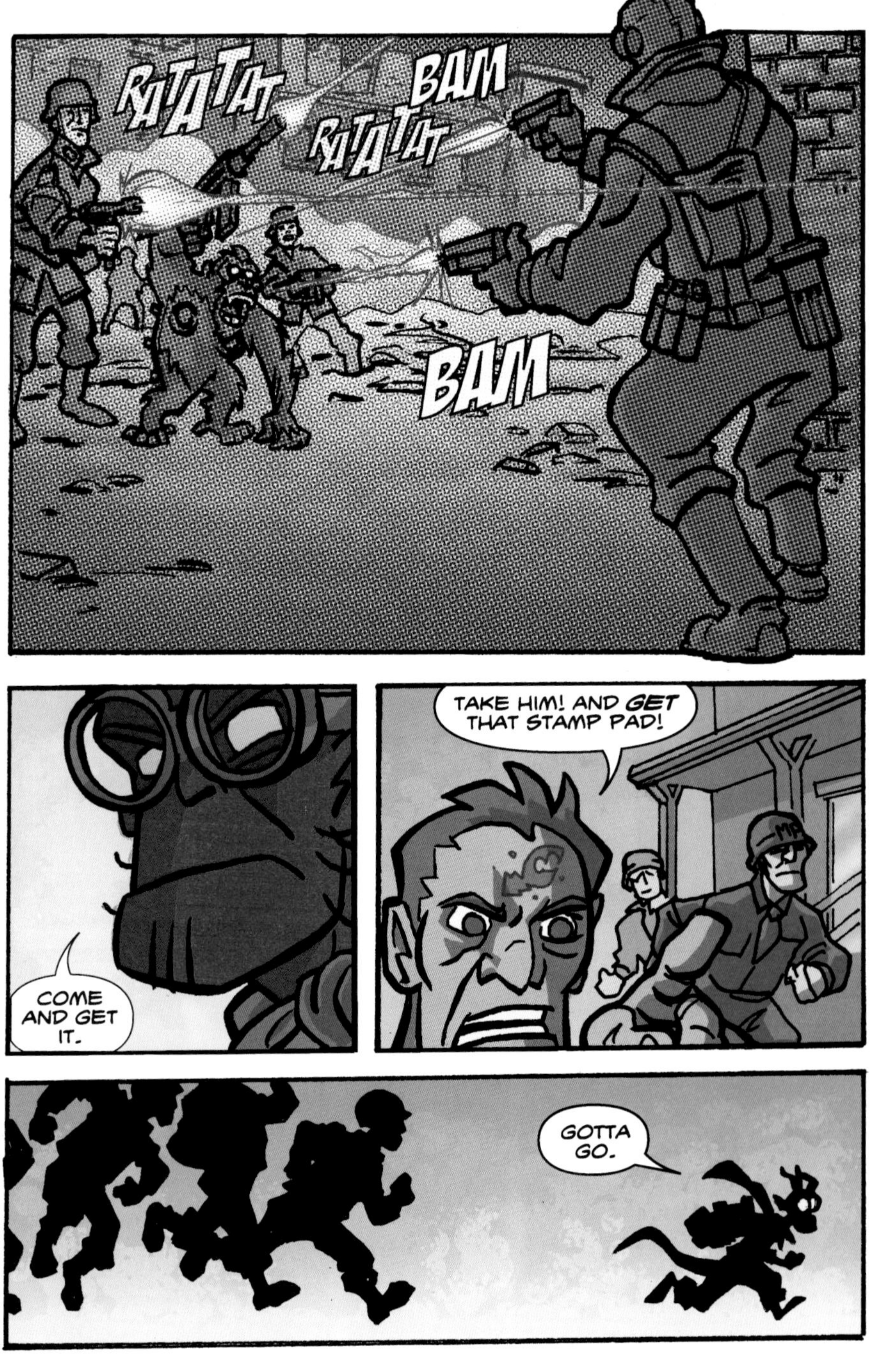
RATATAT
BAM
RATATAT
BAM
COME AND GET IT.
TAKE HIM! AND GET THAT STAMP PAD!
GOTTA GO.

SWEET HEAVENS!

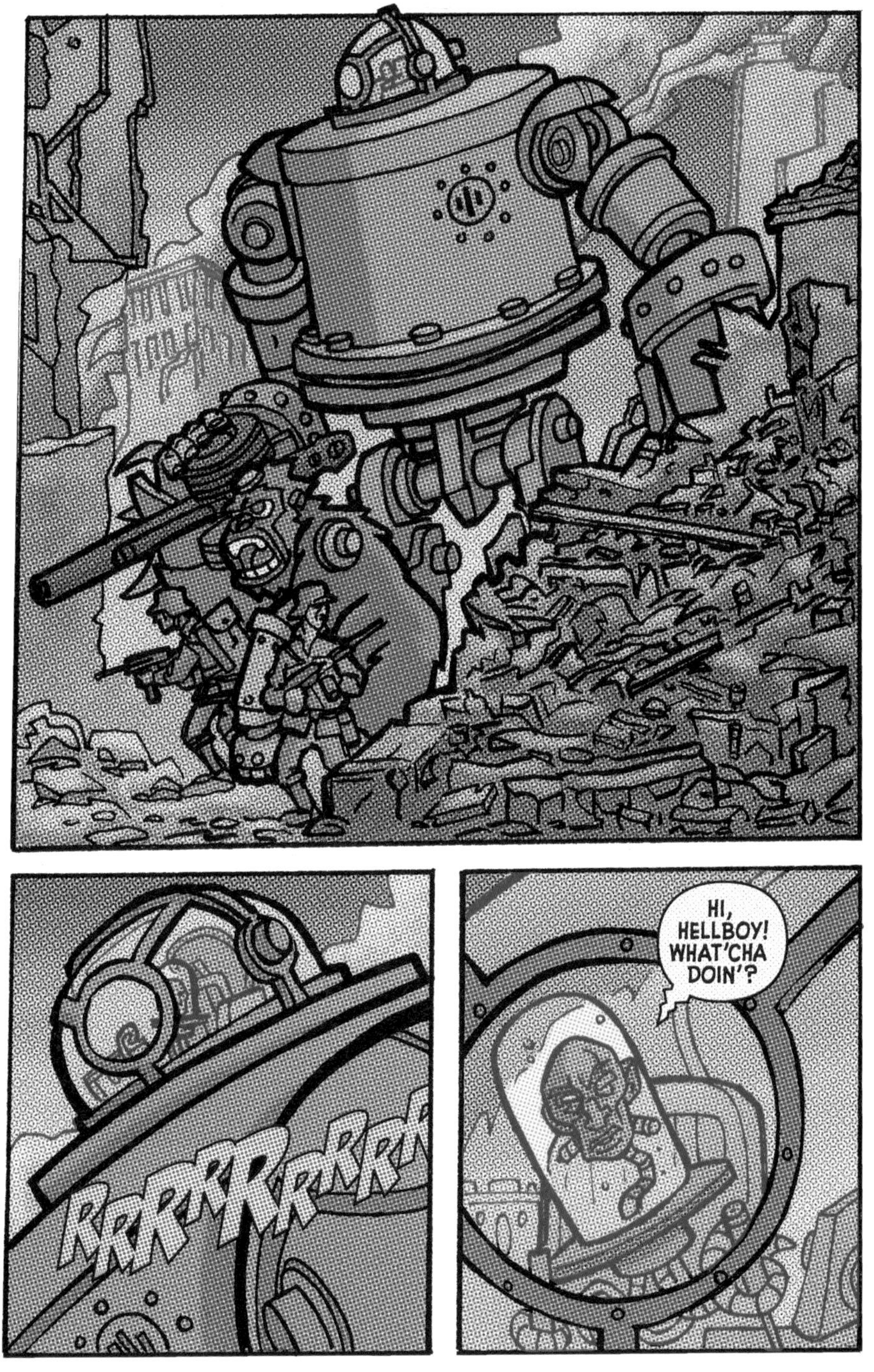
RRRRRRRRRRR
HI, HELLBOY! WHAT'CHA DOIN'?

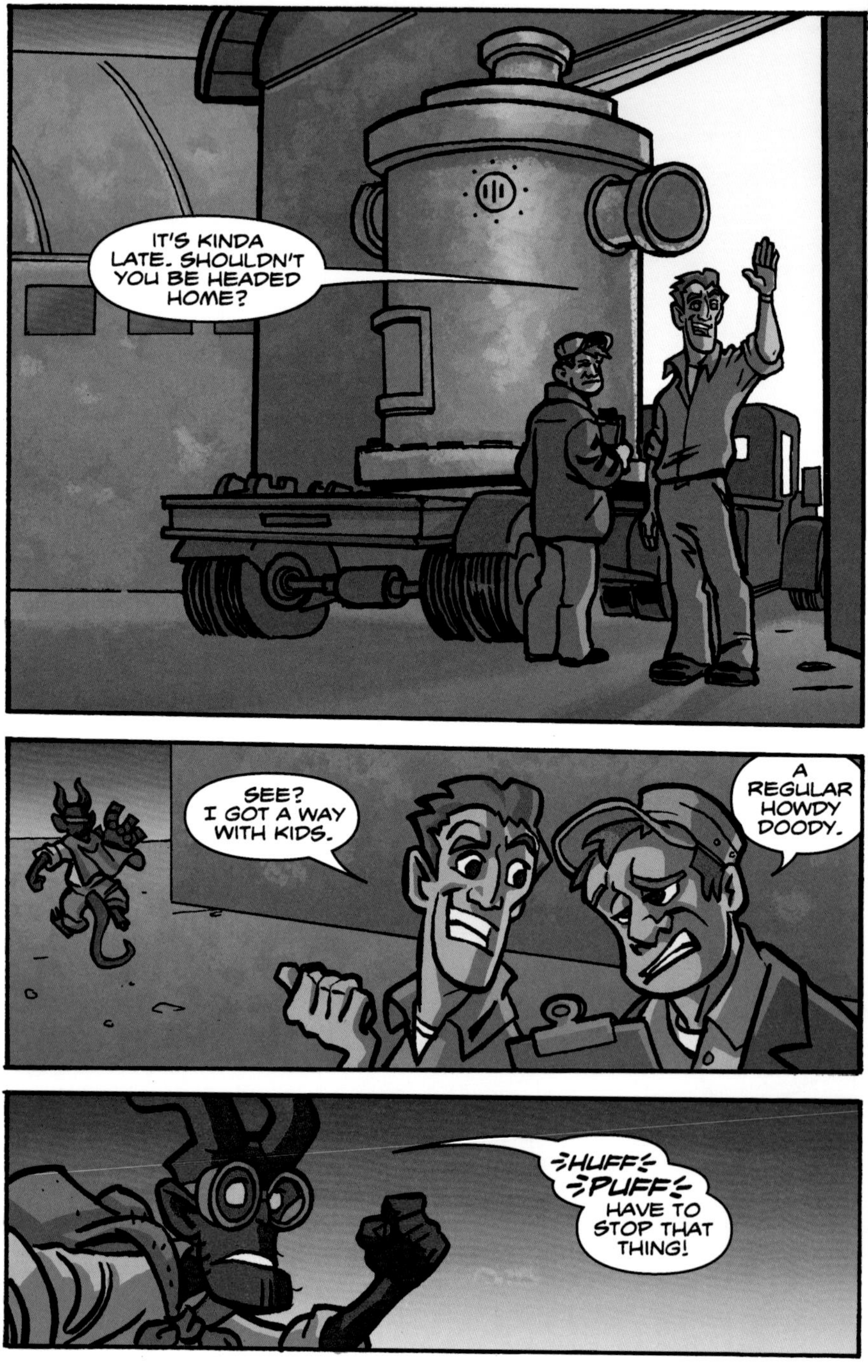
IT'S KINDA LATE. SHOULDN'T YOU BE HEADED HOME?
SEE? I GOT A WAY WITH KIDS.
A REGULAR HOWDY DOODY.
HUFF PUFF HAVE TO STOP THAT THING!

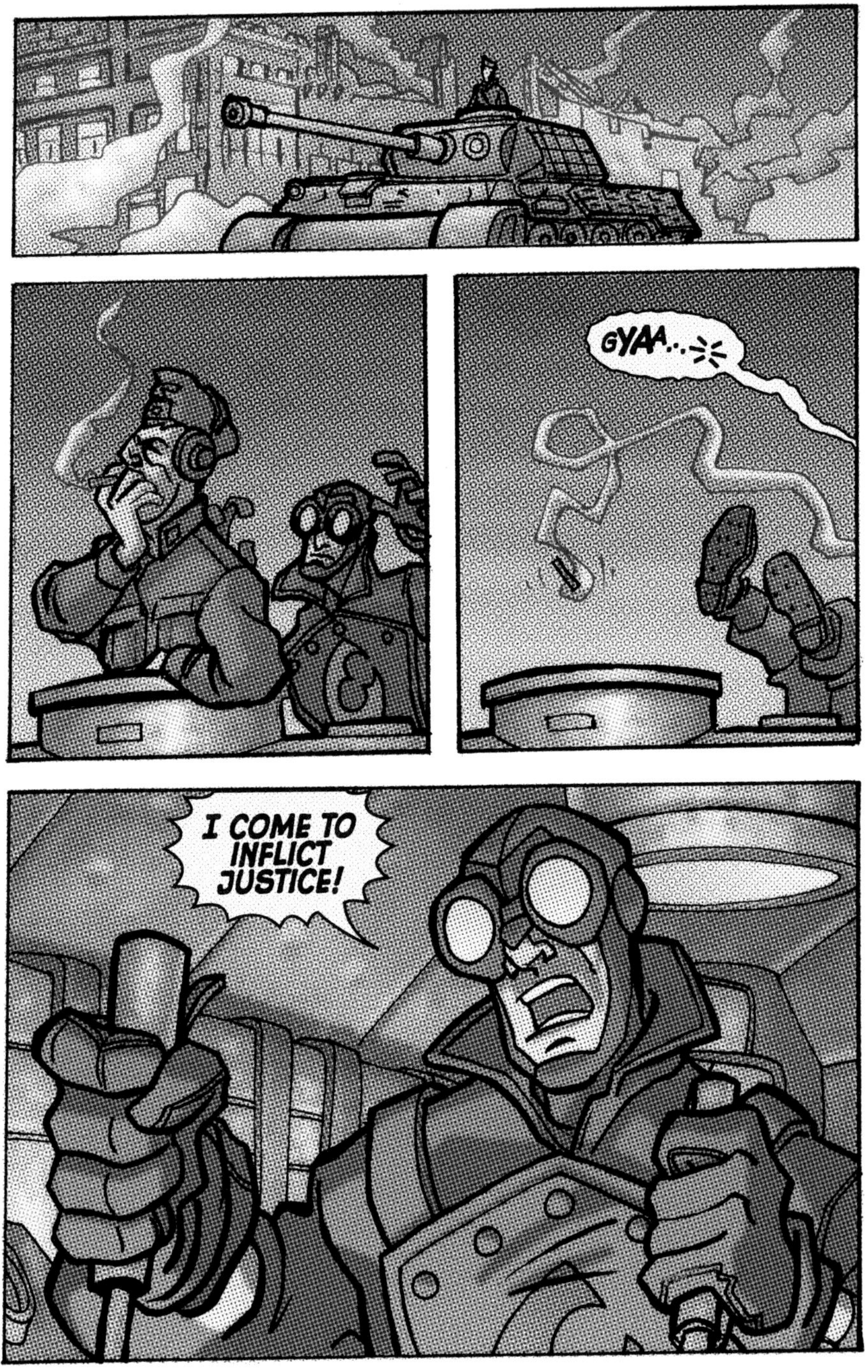
GYAA...
I COME TO INFLICT JUSTICE!

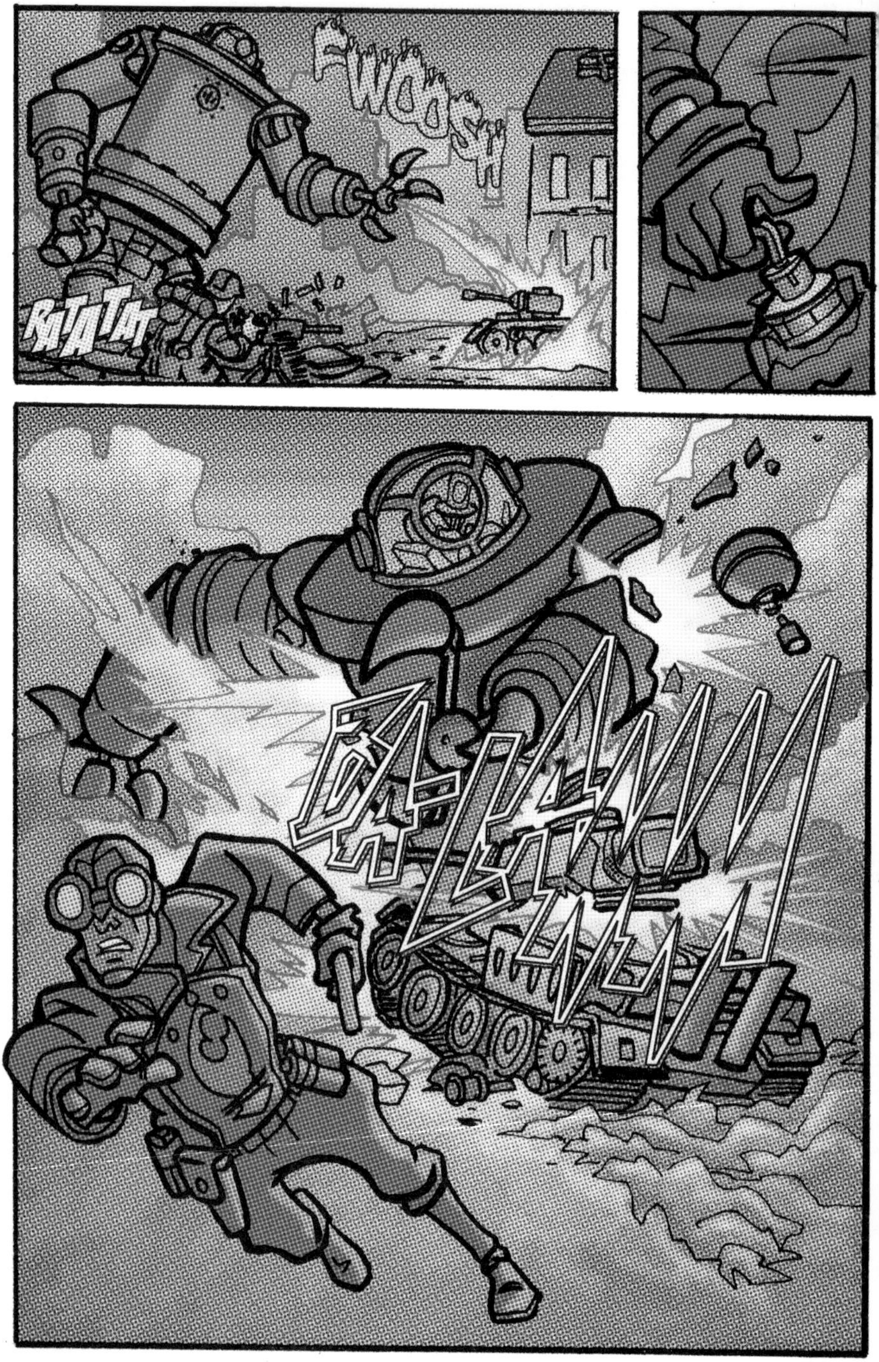
FWOOSH
RATATAT

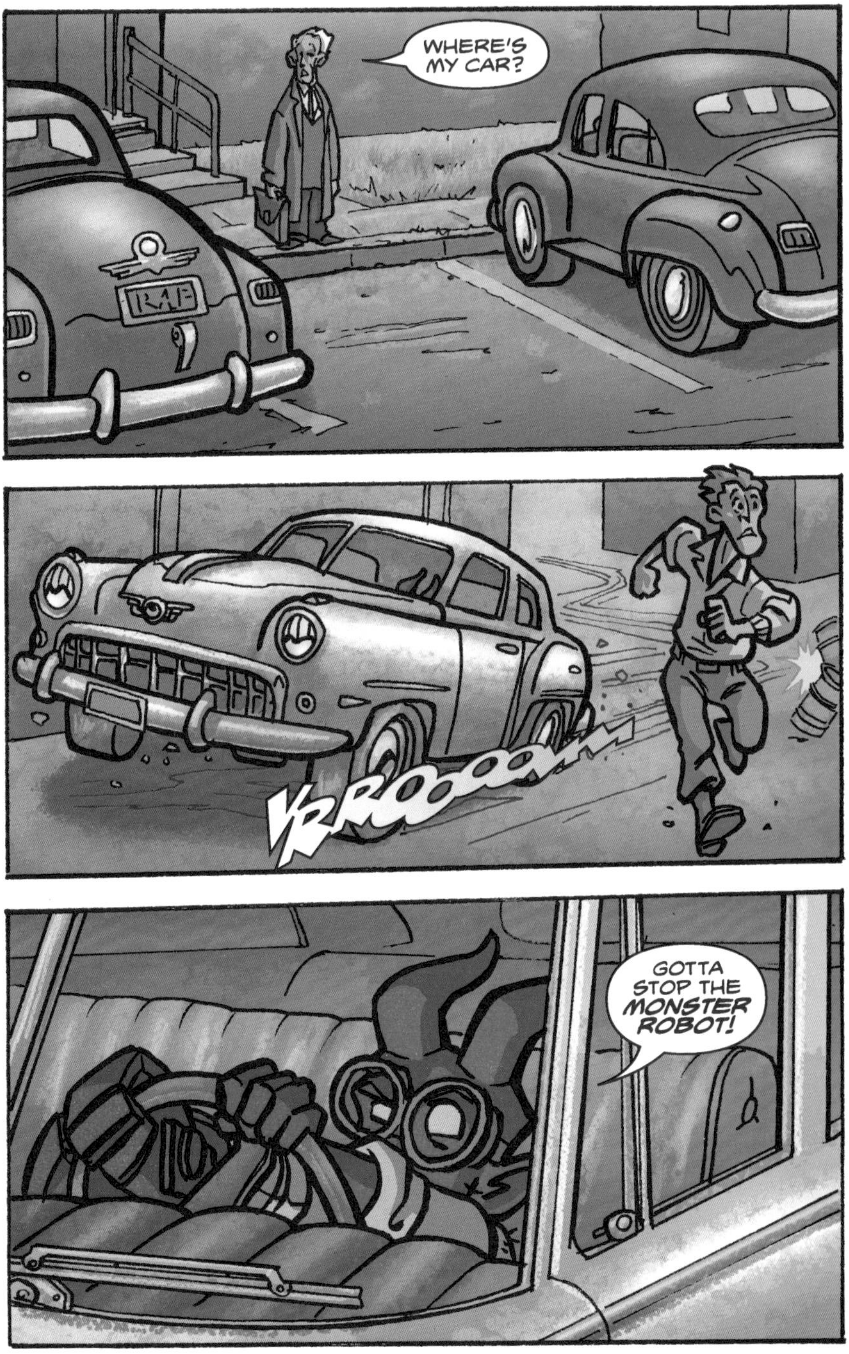
WHERE'S MY CAR?
GOTTA STOP THE *MONSTER ROBOT!*

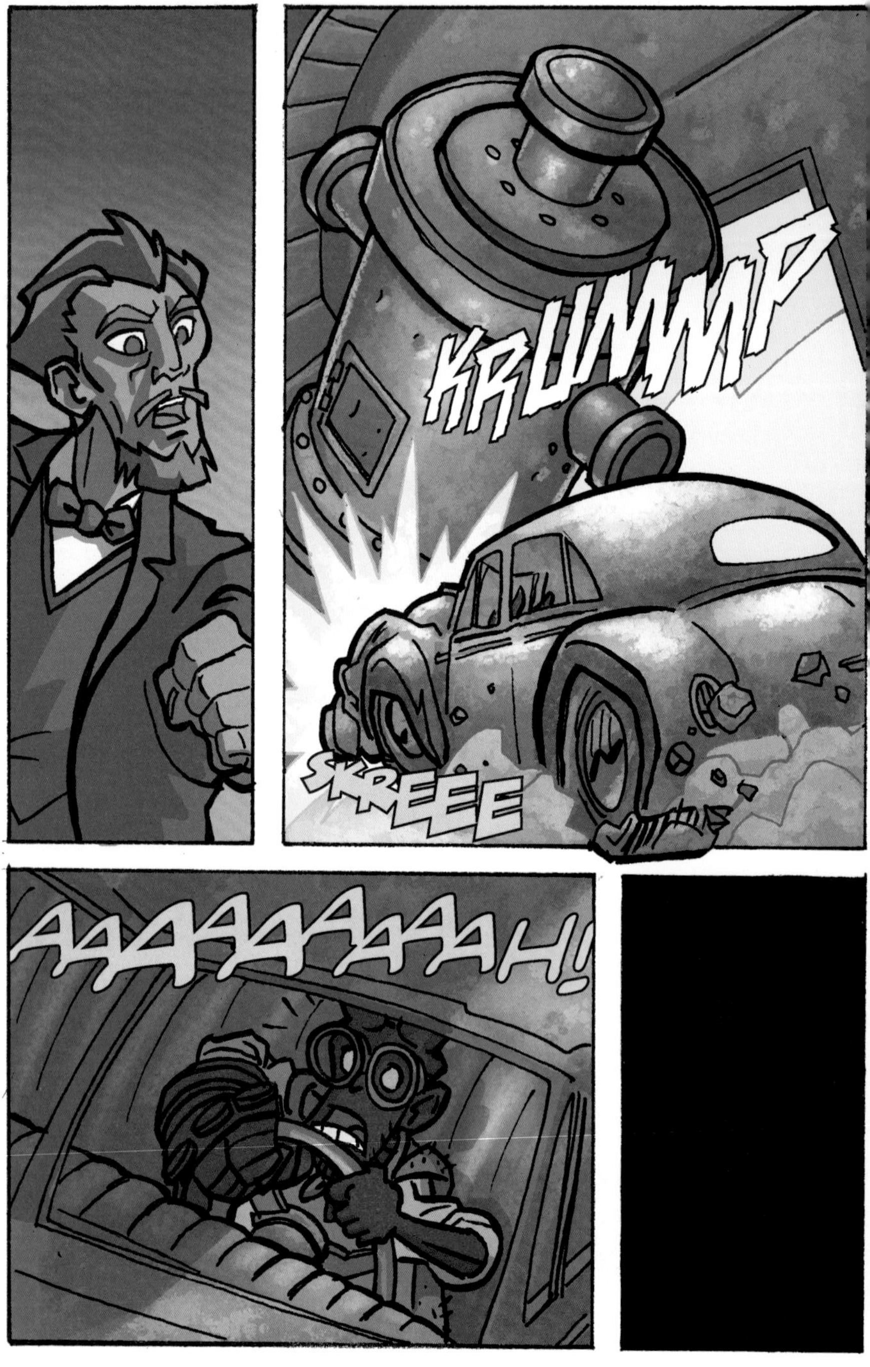
KRUMMP
SKREEEE
AAAAAAAAAH!

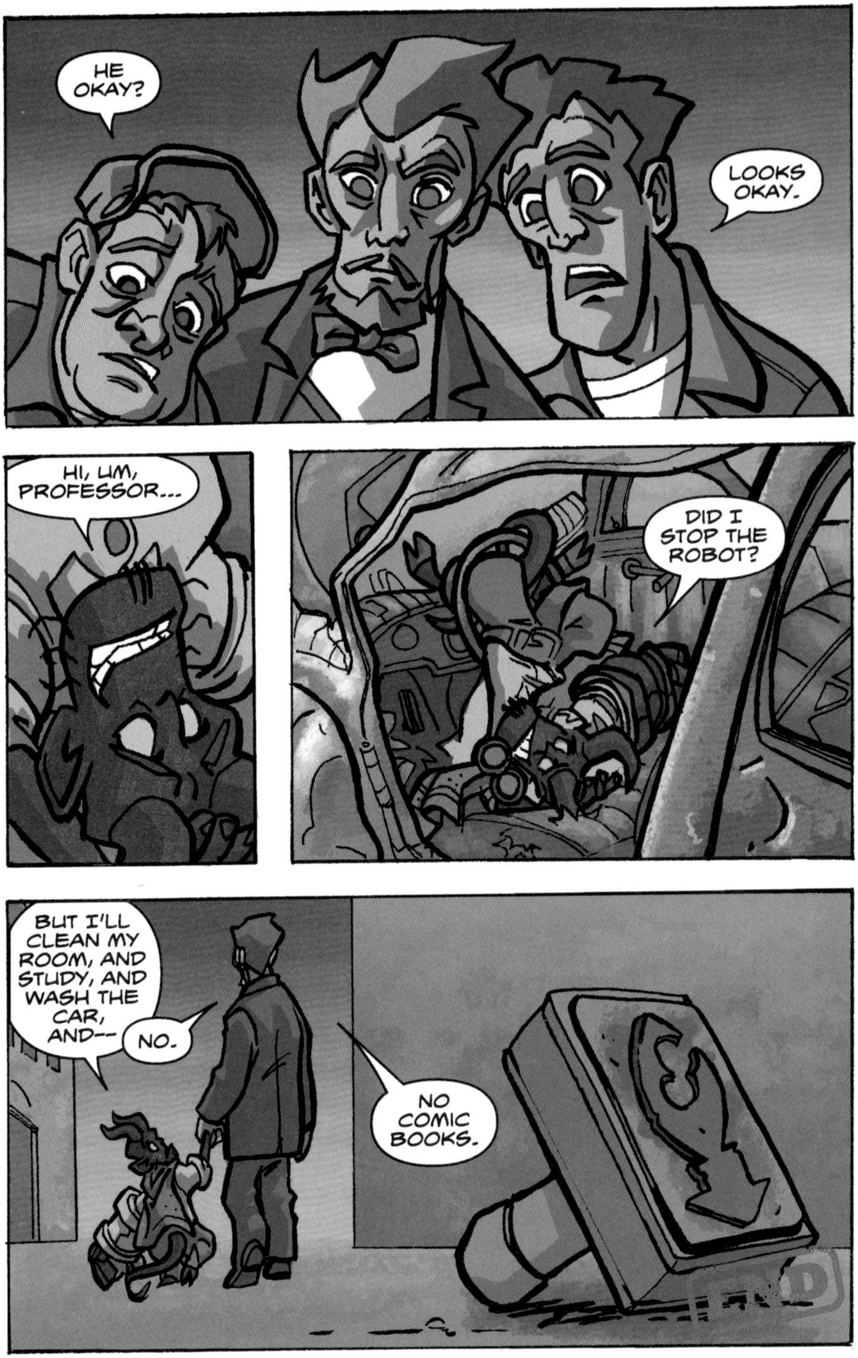
HE OKAY?
LOOKS OKAY.
HI, UM, PROFESSOR...
DID I STOP THE ROBOT?
BUT I'LL CLEAN MY ROOM, AND STUDY, AND WASH THE CAR, AND--
NO.
NO COMIC BOOKS.

ALSO AVAILABLE FROM DARK HORSE

HELLBOY STATUE
10" tall, fully painted statue,
limited edition of 1200 pieces
$150.00

3 PIECE PVC SET
Hellboy, Abe Sapien, & Liz Sherman
$17.99

ABE SAPIEN STATUE
10" tall, fully painted statue,
limited edition of 1200 pieces
$150.00

AVAILABLE AT YOUR LOCAL COMICS SHOP

To find a comics shop in your area, call 1-888-266-4226 For more information
or to order direct visit darkhorse.com or call 1-800-862-0053

DARK HORSE

darkhorse.com   DARK HORSE TWENTY YEARS

COMICS | BOOKS | PRODUCTS | REVIEWS | ZONES | NEWS | HELP | COMPANY | RESOURCES

VISIT THE

ZONE ON DARKHORSE.COM

TO EXPLORE GREAT FEATURES LIKE:

- Exclusive content from editors on upcoming projects!
- Exclusive downloadable desktops!
- Online previews and animations!
- Message Boards!
- Up-to-date information on the latest releases!
- Links to other cool Hellboy sites.

Visit DARKHORSE.COM/HELLBOY for more details!